THE INFLAMMABLE ADAMS

Also by this author

The Unspeakable Adams
More Unspeakable Adams
Uncensored Adams

PHILLIP ADAMS

THE INFLAMMABLE ADAMS

Illustrated by Chris Grosz

NELSON

Thomas Nelson Australia
480 La Trobe Street Melbourne Victoria 3000

First published 1983
Copyright © Phillip Adams 1983
Illustrations copyright © Chris Grosz 1983

National Library of Australia
Cataloguing-in-Publication data:

Adams, Phillip, 1939–.
   The Inflammable Adams.

ISBN 0 17 006316 X.

I. Title.

A824'.3

Typeset in Melbourne by Abb-Typesetting Pty Ltd
Printed in Melbourne by Globe Press

Contents

Foreword by the Hon.
  Mr Justice Michael Kirby, CMG   vii
OK, Adams, what do you believe?   1
'This is Eve. They're trying to kill me.'   8
In the beeswax'd gloom   17
St Anthony's fire   22
King Cheops's royal ship   27
The problem of war begins with hatred   35
My heart goes out to Her Royal Maj   42
On *Gallipoli*   46
Ashton's Circus   51
A final comment on Hitler's diaries   59
The best things to inherit are good genes   63
The Year of the Tree   67
Dramatic compofition fet to mufic   73
The trouble with Bill   77
Kew, Cemetery of the Month   83
A feeling of history   89
Someone to blame   97
Expressing déjà views   103
The world is crawling with Harry Limes   111
Death, or my hobby hearse   115
Bonsai'd bibles and other condensations   118
It's time we did something   121

A flotilla of floats   130
Cases of mistaken identity   133
Let downcasts become outcasts   136
Magnificent maharajahs   140
Island of a million burial mounds   146
Dialogue for the unsuspecting traveller   150
A Magical Memory Tour   157
One Summer of Happiness   162
A morceau of Marceau   167
Butts, barrels and bullets   172
Unidentified flying object   176
High-tech. toys   180
Sugar and spice   184
The all-seeing Patrick White   186
The courtesy of Coward   191
Hitler is still around   193
The unstoppable Zsa Zsa   198
Herpe days   202
Subtitles   205
Vice-Regal vices   208
The Biggest Bang in the Communications Explosion!   211
Confessions of a TV critic   215
A recipe for Adams   219
Gandhi — an *E.T.* for grown-ups   221
Claustrophobia   228

Foreword

Throughout this Foreword I shall refer to him simply as Adams. I elevate him to the mono-nominal ranks — for he is first in our peerage of letters: a dignity I suspect he would not deny, despite the withering descriptions of Vice-Regal vices that appear, hilariously, in this volume.

My first meeting with Adams was typical. We were both attending the inaugural function of a new Federal statutory body to which we had been appointed. There, whilst I was struggling with a cream bun, a cup of tea and my dignity, he thrust himself at my feet, protesting his undying admiration for my every word. 'Am I being sent up?' I dourly asked myself. Or is this doyen of Australia's *literati* really at my feet, going on like this?

Temperance, restraint and decorum are not the strong points of our author. Indeed, I doubt that these sterling, but boring, qualities are to be found in these pages at all. Whether your interests are:

>   the sexuality of male tigers
>   Noel Coward's observations on television
>   the late Arthur Calwell's table manners
>   the gravestones of Kew
>   the Nizam of Hyderabad's huge car collection
>   Johnny Weismuller and the Hoyt's Children's Cinema Club
>   the invention of the guillotine, or
>   Patrick White's egalitarian plane travel

there is something here for everyone, however eccentric. A jumble of history, philosophy and whimsy. And the infuriating thing is that Adams offers the most telling commentary on our country, our world and our times, almost without our noticing it. So complete is Adams's command of the language that he can instruct us with humour, apparently irrelevant facts, an assortment of ideas. And the whole powerful mixture is utterly painless as it does its devilish work.

Why should he invite me to write this Foreword? I must be frank. I asked myself that question when the letter arrived with the thinly veiled suggestion that I should propose him for a Nobel Prize or two. There are really only two Australians who can write Forewords worthy of our author. The first is Dame Edna, another distinguished Melbournian who unaccountably seems to have escaped critical attention in this book.

The other Foreworder First-Class is Gough Whitlam. He wrote the Foreword to *Uncensored Adams* with his usual grace and style — even an allusion or two to Ancient History. Within days of writing that Foreword, the book sold out, the government changed and Mr Whitlam was appointed to an Ambassadorship in Paris, where he is now to be seen again in the corridors of power or basking in the praise of a coterie of admirers in the Rue de Passy. No such happy fate awaits me for this small effort. Indeed, as I write it, I am reflecting on the brothers Maugham. The one, a somewhat stuffy man, went on to become the embroidered Lord Chancellor of All England. The other, a distinctly naughty man, became W. Somerset Maugham. Today, it is the man of letters who is remembered. Creative writing endures when politicians, judges and others have passed on.

In a thousand years or so, when some future civilisation uncovers the wreckage of the National Library, stumbles over the beautifully preserved underground chambers of Parliament House and unearths the ruins of lawyerly pretensions on the banks of Lake Burley Griffin (returned to pasture land) perhaps they will find this book. If they do, what will they make of us? I suspect that they will consider Australians more erudite and well read, self-critical and reflective, than just about any other race on earth. If we must leave our history, let it be this.

And now, Phillip, we are all at your feet. And Here's to a Nobel Prize (or two) for the Inflammable Adams!

Michael Kirby

OK, Adams, what *do* you believe?

OK, Adams, what *do* you believe? I get asked that every week in letters from people who feel snug in this religion, smug in that ideology. First of all I believe, I *know*, that we live on a minor planet in an off-Broadway solar system on the edge of the Milky Way and that, in the final analysis, we're as significant as the eight billionth grain of sand beyond the final palm tree in the most distant oasis in the Sahara. What was Carl Sagan's sandy simile? That there are more suns out there than there are grains of sand on every beach on Earth. From St Kilda to St Tropez. From Elwood to Acapulco.

Consequently, I believe it's absurdly vain to see ourselves as echoing God's image and just as silly to anthropomorphise, to Disneyfy, the concept of God into anything vaguely human. Like the hippopotamus and the hedgehog, humans are simply an evanescent expression of the life force, as destined for oblivion as dodos and dinosaurs.

From early childhood, I've always comprehended, *felt* the immensity of existence, accepted that time and space were infinite, and that the notion of a Creation was a product of mankind's myopia. Being finite creatures ourselves, we wanted to believe in a Beginning, and so we invented a god to begin things. But then any bright six-year-old kid will ask 'But who began God?', bursting that pretty idea like a bubble.

It now appears that there have been many creations, called Big Bangs, that the cosmos comes and goes in a vast, endless oscillation in which the births and deaths of galaxies are of no more consequence than the failures of a few 40-watt light globes.

Therefore, I believe and have always believed that life is totally meaningless and that we have no destiny, no purpose, no author. We just *are*. For a little while, anyway. Then we aren't.

The only meaning life has is subjective, what we care to assign to it as individuals or communities. Rather like people seeing shapes in a Rorschach blot. We cling to these meanings like drowning people to straws. Yet to believe in, for example, the durability of a political idea or the importance of a status symbol, is absurd and self-deceiving. For example, a wrist watch, or a townhall clock, is a useful tool. But in the context of infinite time the watch and the clock are travesties.

It's much the same with morality. Morals are simply expedients, rules that we set up like traffic lights to try to sort things out. To prevent collisions. To keep things moving along in a fairly orderly fashion. Most of the time I obey traffic lights, but I'm damned if I'll sit at a red light at 3 o'clock in the morning, the only car at an intersection. Ditto with 'moral' regulations. Thus while I'm opposed to violence and hostile to capital punishment, I can easily envisage circumstances where I *could* kill (others, or myself) without moral qualms. Clearly, if you live in a universe where there's no meaning, there is, finally, no absolute morality.

I believe that what we call love is a useful social adhesive that, much of the time, stops things falling apart. I believe that the loves of man for woman, parent for child, and friend for friend are not enormously different — they're variations on a theme involving yearning, loneliness, possessiveness, sexuality and fear that gives humans some of their best and worst moments. Best *and* worst. That's something else I believe in very, very strongly. In paradox and contradiction.

Thus I cannot believe that the truth is always good. It isn't necessarily good to tell someone who's dying that they're dying or someone who's ugly that they're ugly. Sometimes it's far, far better to lie.

I also recognise the paradox of emotion, having found that, when I'm most intensely happy, I am, in that same moment, almost equally sad. You might be watching your kids running around the garden laughing and exultant, and you're conscious that that instant is already becoming a memory, like a fading photograph. Great composers recognise such complexities in their music, just as Shakespeare put the Monty Pythonesque Porter's scene in the middle of *Macbeth*. Just as Chaplin intensified his comedy with elements of the tragic.

I believe that we live by delusions — ranging from temporal self-importance to the fatuous notion of everlasting life. To live without such delusions is, I must say, pleasantly liberating. It gives you a sense of recklessness and freedom that most people, locked in their belief systems, lack. Yet there are times when I wish I *did* believe in some prepackaged faith or philosophy because it would make life easier. And I've observed many circumstances in which such delusions have, for the dying or the bereaved, made death easier.

Speaking of paradox, I saw a documentary film a few months ago that began with a lingering close-up of one of the most beautiful human faces I've ever seen. It *had* to be the face of a saint. Unfortunately it wasn't. It was the face of one of the most savage torturers of the Greek colonel's regime. He's now repentant but for years he turned dissidents into screaming maniacs and, in many cases, into vegetables. And he served to remind me that, under certain circumstances, almost all of us are capable of monstrous cruelty.

As a child, I was deeply moved by a collection of photographs called *The Family of Man* in which quotations from great literature gave added meaning to the images. In that book, one phrase had particular power: 'Nothing that is human is alien to me'. I believe that wholeheartedly and have rarely felt moral superiority. About anybody.

Another paradox. I like the energy of capitalism yet deplore its lack of social justice. I admire the compassion of socialism while deploring its tendency to bureaucratise. If only you could combine the energy of one with the idealism of the other.

I'm not a Luddite — finding technology enthralling and seeing the *Concorde* as beautiful as a Gothic cathedral. I despise superstition of all sorts because of the way it makes people capitulate to the dictates of charlatans. On the other hand, I love the way humans fantasise and imagine, and would place no limit on such imaginings. While believing that we should teach Mystery as well as History, Myths as well as Maths, I'd prefer people to differentiate between their fantasies and their lives.

Yet I believe that religions are nonsensical and, for me, completely unnecessary. Many of the troubles on this planet flow from the factional fictions that men call Faith. Whether they're Christians mowing down Moslems for which Jews get the blame, or Catholics carving up Protestants or white South Africans using the Bible as their justification for apartheid. If we *must* have religions, why not revert to good, old-fashioned pantheism? Or Sun worship? But as I often say to people who write me angry letters about religion, 'Let's not let a little thing like God come between us'.

I'm unconcerned by what people do to themselves, or each other, sexually. That is, provided it doesn't involve force or bullying. (Even then, there are circumstances where people *like* to be forced and bullied and that's OK too.) In other words, I believe in tolerance provided it doesn't become indifference just as I believe in scepticism provided it doesn't become cynicism.

Some aspects of human affairs should be *very* organised. Such as keeping our air and water clean. At the same time, I think we should allow people to wear what they like and do what they like — even if what they like involves foolishness or danger. There are times when it seems that paternalism in society is almost as bad as totalitarianism. There ought to be a law against too many laws.

I believe in laughter. A highly developed sense of the absurd, particularly of one's own absurdity, is extremely healthy. As long as you're laughing, especially at yourself, you're unlikely to be brutal or vindictive. I think that all the things we use to divide us — from brands of god to national borders — are fairly silly and should be laughed at as often as possible. Yet — another paradox — the things that divide us create a cultural diversity that's endlessly fascinating. While it would be splendid to have the world united as recommended in some of the nobler folk songs, there's something to be said for a world that contrasts Trobriand Islanders with Texans, pigmies with Watusis and Quexacotal Indians with Queenslanders.

Progress? I've long believed that for every step forward there's one step back, that the answer to every social problem creates a new problem, that change is exhilarating and yet, in many ways, illusory. But that complacent platitude may be running out of time as, in the next few years, our geneticists and electronic whiz kids will begin to toss away the past.

I believe that life is very short and, if there's such a thing as blasphemy, it's wasting it. As we only live once, I believe in living as many lives as possible within the miserable allocation allotted to us by genetics and circumstance. I believe that most of the big questions don't have answers and the people who think they *do* have answers are either fools or dangerous. Particularly if they reduce their answers to slogans.

I think we're particularly lucky to be alive at this moment, that we're standing on an historic hilltop with quite spectacular views. We can see a long way into the past and some distance into the future. We can enjoy cave paintings and comic strips, the architecture of Venice and Frank Lloyd Wright. There's a smorgasbord of ideas and experiences available to us that man has never known until this century, indeed this decade. We can eat lots of foods and go to lots of places — and if one of those places is the dentist, it doesn't hurt so much these days. Moreover, since the 1940s, medicine has started to mean something.

I find I hold opposing views on almost every subject and don't think there's anything much wrong with that. Truth is composed of opposing views as surely as air is composed of oxygen, hydrogen and some other stuff I can't remember. It's as if everyone in the world had a piece of a jigsaw puzzle and that, from time to time, a few pieces fitted together and we saw a little piece of the picture.

I think that most of the things that occupy our minds are sound and fury that signify nothing. The moving finger writes and having writ moves on and all that sort of thing. I believe that beauty celebrates life, and ugliness, by and large, has to do with death. I've met enough of the great and the mighty to know that they tend to be remarkably ordinary. I believe that most of the really extraordinary things men have done have been completely dotty — like building pyramids, cathedrals and Eiffel Towers. These silly, theatrical gestures are an unconscionable waste of everyone's time and money, yet where would we be without them? Obviously we should actively encourage such stupidities recognising that rationality tends to produce office blocks and highrise buildings.

If there was a god, which there isn't, you'd have to acknowledge his perversity in that almost everything we like doing, whether that involves eating or sex, is naughty. Which reminds me of something else I believe — that obscenity in a Rabelaisian or Chaucerian sense is very healthy whilst pornography is a product of sexual repression. It's men like the Reverend Fred Nile who are the true pornographers.

In the end I don't believe in believing. It's interesting to think and to speculate and to come to tentative conclusions which you're willing to review and revise on an almost hourly basis. As soon as you lock something away as a belief, it's like putting a thought into prison. That's what I like about science, so far as I understand it. Science mounts hypotheses and, if they seem to work out, goes along with them. Yet nobody minds in the slightest if it turns out that the hypotheses were wrong. Thus, I believe in believing in as little as possible, particularly if belief involves signing a manifesto.

My favourite characters are men like Diogenes who knew about absurdity and paradox and hated the pompous and the arrogant. Which is why I'm not all that enamoured of your Brezhnevs and Reagans as I certainly don't believe that *anything* is worth having a nuclear war about. For my own part, I'd happily surrender to the first country that undertook to unleash one as it's patently absurd for a man who lives in Pennsylvania Avenue, Washington, to destroy the planet because he disagrees with another old man who lives across the brick-paved courtyard from the Hotel Russia. To blow up the world over their minor differences is as grotesque and unreasonable as, well, defoliating the jungles of the Amazon because the president of Brazil has hayfever.

Action and reaction, positive and negative, thesis and antithesis, rule and exception, life and death. To be sane involves embracing opposites and accepting contradictions. It also involves accepting the reality of death without being afraid of it. And how can we fear something that we know so well? For we've all been dead already. We know what death looks, feels and smells like because we've all been dead for billions of years. If you want to know what death's like, just think back a few years to before you were born. Death's exactly the same thing.

'This is Eve. They're trying to kill me.'

The phone rings when I'm in the final furlong of Friday afternoon. Trying to hold two meetings simultaneously whilst, at the same time, shuffling papers into a briefcase. Irritated by the umpteenth interruption, I answer it brusquely. 'This is Eve', says a woman, obviously calling from a public phone. 'They're trying to kill me.'

Eve? Do I know an Eve? Putting a hand over the mouthpiece, I call out to my secretary — 'Who the hell's Eve?' She doesn't know either.

The people in my office are talking, laughing, so I signal for some ssshhh. 'Yes Eve, what's the problem?'

'You'll have to help me, or they'll kill me.'
'Who's they?'
A silence.
'Where are you, Eve?'
'I can't tell you that. I want to come to your office.'
'I'm sorry Eve, but I'm in the middle of a couple of meetings and will have to leave almost immediately. If you tell me where you are or who's trying to hurt you, I'll see if I can help.'
Another silence.
'Look, how can I help you, if you won't tell me anything?'
'I'm too frightened.'
'Well, I suggest you come and see me first thing on Monday morning.'
'I'll be dead by then.'
She hangs up.

In an average week I get a dozen ratbag calls. And ten, twenty strange people will suddenly appear in my office to tell their stories or ask for help. You learn to be cautious, sceptical. But there's something about Eve's voice that makes me feel guilty and ashamed. In my eagerness to escape the office I may have been careless with her life. But the meetings pick up where they left off, and Eve goes into the Out basket.

Then, on Monday morning, one of the most beautiful women I've ever seen appears in my office. She is tall, seems to be in her mid-20s, and her long blonde hair is tangled and dirty. She's wearing cheap, op-shop clothes and her bare legs are scratched and torn. Her eyes are blue, intelligent and frightened.

'I'm Eve', she says.

She has a friend with her, a stocky, bearded man of indeterminate age wearing a heavy woollen jumper and a knitted hat. If anything, he looks more afraid than Eve. In the next 30 minutes he says absolutely nothing, lets her do all the talking. But before she makes a comment or answers a question, they'll exchange long glances. It's as if he's giving her silent directions, secret permissions. She introduces him as Adam.

Extracting information is like pulling teeth. The two seem

terrified of revealing anything, lest I betray them to their enemies.

Eve reveals that there's a pram in the foyer containing twin babies. 'Don't tell me they're Cain and Abel?' I grin. Not seeing the joke, she shakes her head, and gives me other names. Saul and David. The New South Wales police have pursued the four of them halfway across Australia. They want to put Adam in prison, her in a mental home and give the babies to her mother. But she's convinced that her mother will kill them. Just as she's trying to have Adam killed. For as well as the police, they're being hunted by men hired by her parents who have opened fire on them on two occasions already. She shows me her torn legs and tells of a terrifying night when they'd fled a country town and run, stumbling through the bush, for hour after hour. Chased by her mother's hired killers.

They'd been hiding out for months in small country towns. For a time they'd stayed in a commune at Nimbin but, even there, someone had betrayed them. The police had arrived in a helicopter and they'd had to hide in the bush, in the darkness. She trembles as she relives the horrors of that night.

Now Adam wheels a battered, wobbly pram into my office. It contains two very young babies, oddly bound in rags. Are these what they call swaddling clothes? Suddenly the image of Joseph and Mary enters my head, just as I'm sure it was meant to. Joseph and Mary with *two* holy infants, hotly pursued by murderous authority.

Eve breast-feeds one of the babies while I question her about her past. Refusing to give me any specific information that would enable me to identify her or her parents, she says she was brought up in a wealthy Sydney home, had gone to the best schools, had been a champion athlete and had a job in an expensive boutique. That she'd loved her loving parents in what had seemed the best of all possible worlds. Then she'd met Adam, poet and philosopher, and fallen deeply in love. At first her parents had been friendly but then had turned against them, driving Adam away. She'd followed him, become pregnant and had the twins. Her mother had told lies about Adam to the police, convincing them that he was a monster and that she,

Eve, had become mentally unstable because of drugs. And as if the police weren't enough, her mother had also hired private detectives and a couple of criminals.

The image of Joseph and Mary fades and, looking at Adam, I wonder whether I'm not in fact looking at Charles Manson. Now I begin addressing all my questions to him and forcing the odd monosyllabic response. He tells me that he's been a professional fisherman for many years, using the solitude to think and write. Finally I persuade him to open a haversack and show me some of his poems. The torn exercise books he passes me confirm my suspicions. The poems are pretentious and portentous, full of cosmic gobbledygook and transcendental cliché. They are full of familiar paranoia in which the author claims a special and unique vision and details his loathing for a corrupt and doomed society. More significantly, he seems to be claiming quite extraordinary, god-like wisdom. The poems are written in different coloured pens (something I often note in the loonier letters we get) and seem to be by any number of hands.

'But Adam, many people have written these.'

'No, I wrote them all.'

'Some of these poems are signed Thundercloud', I observe.

'Some people call me that', says Adam.

I've seen this sort of material before, from mental patients. There's no doubt in my mind that Adam is obsessed and unstable, possibly to the point of madness. But, if anything, that tends to confirm Eve's story.

Not that anyone looking into Eve's extraordinarily beautiful face and eyes could doubt that she believed everything she was telling me. Nor could you doubt her devotion to Adam and her babies. And one could well believe that her mother, frantic with anxiety, had become unbalanced. After all, Adam (or Thundercloud) wasn't exactly Bellevue Hill's idea of the perfect son-in-law. Anything alleged about him, to police, would seem credible.

Well, what can I do for them? If Eve tells me her real name or her parents' names, I will ring them and try to intervene on her behalf. If she likes, I'll speak to the Attorney-General in New South Wales and ask him to call off the police. Eve looks at Adam for a long time. Then, turning to me, she shakes her head. No, they are afraid that they'll be captured or separated. Or her mother's gunmen will get to them first.

What do they want of me then? Simply a few hundred dollars so that they can go and hide in the bush again. I scoff at the suggestion. A tall, beautiful blonde, a bearded dwarf and two babies would be rather noticeable in a country town. If you want to hide, you'll be safer in the city.

Trying to take the initiative I make the following offers. I will speak to the Attorney-General and put their side of the story. I will put them in touch with one of the best lawyers in Victoria who will give them unlimited free advice. I will arrange through my social welfare connections to have them sheltered and I will also get Adam a job.

Adam says that he won't leave Eve and the babies for a minute, so the job is out of the question. But yes, they will speak to my lawyer and they'd be grateful for the shelter. While they sit there I make the necessary phone calls, letting them hear everything I say to the lawyer and the social worker. 'I believe a lot of what they're telling me. I think they're genuinely afraid and that they're in some sort of danger. But I'm not convinced by everything they're telling me. There are aspects of the yarn that are very hard to swallow.'

I ring off. Adam and Eve know that nothing has been said behind their backs. Now I give them some money and a taxi docket and they agree to see the social worker first, and then the lawyer.

I take them downstairs, helping fold the pram into the boot of the taxi. Adam grasps my hands and tries to thank me but appears overwhelmed with emotion. Eve looks nervously around at the passing traffic, at people on the footpath.

A few hours later the social worker rings me and says that he, too, was impressed with Eve's honesty and tended to believe most of her story. Like me, he's convinced that Adam is unstable. But that doesn't give anyone, even Eve's parents, the right to hunt them down like animals. Apart from any other consideration, the tactic was counter-productive. All the parents had succeeded in doing was bonding them together. He'd given them the address of a refuge where they'd be fed and sheltered and offered Adam work which, once again, he'd refused. They'd then gone off to see my lawyer.

But they never arrive. Nor do they arrive at the refuge. I hear nothing from them for two days and am afraid for them both. Yet somehow I feel it would be wrong to phone the police. Then, suddenly, they're in my office again. Eve apologises for their disappearance, explaining that they were simply too afraid to go to the refuge or to the lawyer.

I'm angry, saying that they shouldn't have returned if they don't trust me. That I was doing my best to help them and they were making it bloody impossible. Once again I ask for the parents' name.

No, says Eve, I don't want to get them into trouble. I don't want to hurt them any more than they've been hurt already. Her sudden solicitude seems strange and inconsistent. As is her next suggestion — that I buy the rights to their story for the *Age*. Now I burst out laughing. You don't want to hurt your mother and yet you want to tell the whole story in the newspapers? In any case, I explain, no newspaper would run the story without checking the facts.

Once again I offer to negotiate a truce. It's Adam's turn to laugh — a truce with people who are trying to kill him? Once again they beg me for money so that they can buy a used car and simply disappear. Once again I say that such an extraordinary foursome could hardly disappear, that they'd be as conspicuous as Martians wherever they went. I repeat that I'm willing to give them financial help on *condition* that they speak to my lawyer. Once again there are long silences with Eve searching Adam's face for minutes at a time before making any further comment.

I suddenly realise that she is being controlled by Adam, that she's become a sort of lovely ventriloquial doll speaking only with his permission. More and more Adam-Thundercloud is evoking memories of Manson. Having three daughters myself — and having seen what cults and cultists can do to kids —

Eve's parents have some of my sympathy.

I interrogate the pair for hours, trying to get one clue that will enable me to make contact with the parents, however cautiously. But it's an impasse. Finally I tell them to go. 'If you won't trust me, I can't help you. You're on your own.'

As they leave, Eve turns to me imploringly. 'I'm telling you the truth. Paul would tell you.' Paul who? But she refuses to be drawn out — it's as if she's said too much already.

After they've gone I wonder about Paul. Clearly he is somebody I know. A mutual friend. Presumably he lives in Sydney. Paul who? I only know one Paul. He works for me in my Sydney office. So I phone him and tell him the extraordinary story. Does it ring a bell? Does it mean anything to him? No, it doesn't.

An hour later he rings me back. He vaguely remembers hearing a story about a girl, a friend of his wife's, who had left her family for some superannuated beatnik. He gives me a surname and a suburb.

Moments later I'm talking to Eve's mother who, far from sounding like a killer, weeps with joy. 'You mean she's *alive*! Oh my God, we thought she was dead. We've heard nothing from her for two years.'

'Look, I can't tell you where they are. I gave my word that I wouldn't reveal their whereabouts. I'm just ringing you to say that she and the babies are OK.'

'Babies?' She's obviously astonished to hear of the kids. I hear her call out to her husband relaying the information. I hear his cry of astonishment. Realising that Eve has told me less than the truth, I tell the mother of the accusations about private detectives and hit-men.

Taking it in turns to hold the telephone, both she and her husband assure me that it's nonsense. Of course they'd been aghast when their daughter had turned up with Thundercloud, the name he'd been using then. But they'd done their best to cope, to make him welcome. As the months passed, they'd seen less and less of them — and what they did see caused them great distress. He was starving the girl, arguing the psychic benefits of some crazed diet. Apart from losing an enormous amount of weight, she'd lost her ability to reason. He'd become more and more dominating until it got to a point where she seemed to be under his mental control, as though in a state of hypnosis.

This, of course, confirms what I'd observed. And I know that a starvation diet is often used by cults to facilitate mind control.

Finally, they'd disappeared and for two years the parents had heard nothing.

We had lost our third child, says the mother. And now it is her story, not Eve's, that is impossible to believe. 'Firstly our little boy died of leukemia. Secondly Jill's sister was killed in a car accident. We believed that those tragedies, apart from destroying our health, undermined Jill's. That having been brilliant at school and at sport and full of confidence for her life, those deaths had undermined her psychologically. Just as they did with her father and me. Dad had to retire from his business just to help me survive.'

It turns out that Thundercloud is well known to the police. He had many aliases in many states and a long criminal record. Now, convinced that the world was to be destroyed by nuclear war, he's decided to find his own Garden of Eden and to begin repopulating the planet. Their daughter had been chosen for a signal honour.

I explain to the parents that even so I cannot help them find their daughter. Apart from any other consideration I don't know where she is. Yet even if she was sitting in my office in front of me, all I'd do would be to ask her to talk to them on the telephone. I say that Eve passionately believes everything she says to me — hence her ability to make others believe. And that the only hope they have of seeing their daughter again is for her relationship with Adam to disintegrate. They agree, and say they're deeply grateful to know that she's alive and looking well.

'And you say she looks beautiful again', says the mother.

'Very.'

'That's marvellous to hear. She looked like a ghost the last time we saw her.'

I tell the parents that I doubt I'll be hearing from Adam and

Eve again, but if they make contact, I'll try to persuade Eve to phone.

A few minutes later they do make contact, but this time it's Adam who does the talking. In his cunning, he realised that Eve's reference to Paul had been a giveaway and that by now I may have pieced the truth together. So there's no way he'll allow Eve to talk to me. Once again, I can tell they're calling from a public booth, yet when I ask to speak to Eve, he says she isn't there. 'But you never leave her alone, Adam. You're too afraid to leave her for a moment.' He makes no response.

Finally I do my block. I tell Adam that I know the whole story is a fabrication, that Jill is simply a puppet under his control — and that I'll do anything in my power to save her from him. My outburst is, of course, stupid. He curses me and hangs up.

I phone Jill's parents and suggest there's one way to put the relationship under pressure. If we make the story public, as public as possible, they couldn't travel anywhere without being identified. Nor will anyone believe Eve's story, no matter how brilliantly she tells it. Adam can only operate in the shadows, in darkness and mystery. Exposed to the light, his poisonous fantasies will wither. And perhaps, just perhaps, appeals from her mother will get through to Eve. I've already spoken to Gerald Stone of *60 Minutes* and we can get the story into scores of newspapers and magazines. Yes, it will mean even more pain for the parents but there's some small hope for a reconciliation. On the other hand, there are considerable dangers — that trapped in the spotlight of publicity, Adam will be even more dangerous. The parents say they'll consider it and phone me back. When they do, they choose silence. To wait in hope.

All this happened 18 months ago. Hardly a week has gone by when I haven't remembered the beautiful face of that tragic girl. Or the plight of two decent, caring parents who lost three children. One to terminal illness, one to a road accident, and one to the age of Aquarius.

In the beeswax'd gloom

Loathing high-tech decor, with its plexiglass ornaments and nose-cone furniture (sometimes it's hard to tell a house from a dentist's surgery), I prefer to soothe my senses in the beeswax'd gloom of the antique shop, amongst the mellow, tenth-hand flotsam of the centuries, where objects have mystery instead of mere utility if they have any utility at all.

Every Saturday morning for twenty years I did the rounds, starting at Archie Mears whom you'd find amidst his subtle, understated stock reflectively smoking a cigar, and finishing with Godfrey Hayes who could convince a sceptical Cardinal that a broken rung from a builder's ladder was a piece of the One True Cross. (I once heard him tell a dowager that a very ordinary couch was stuffed with the feathers from the swans of St Petersburg, the very birds that inspired Tchaikovsky to write *Swan Lake*.)

I met people who could turn a laminex table into a 16th century refectory table from a Balkan monastery by smearing it with Kiwi and belting it with bike chains, finally authenticating it with a British Antique Dealer's Gold Seal lifted from a walnut Davenport with a razor blade. Combining the sincerity of the clergy with the rapaciousness of the used car dealer, these antique double-dealers were the most enchanting of villains.

Mind you, the profession has its authentic aristocracy. The dour John Dunn who deals in admirable oak and the odd, grim carving of a saint from Gothic Germany. Mr Broadway, late of George's, who sold me the grandfather clock that's ticked quietly, ominously in the hall for the last twenty-five years. The Austrian baroness in Chapel Street (though I prefer to pretend that she's really Crown Princess Anastasia) whose sad, sweet face shines with joy as she shows you a favourite Persian rug or a lugubrious oil painting.

There's big Bill Johnson who has the Governor's brother to dust his ruby chandeliers, and who seems determined never to sell anything. Even if you do persuade him to accept a cheque,

17

he's most reluctant to deliver the goods. As far as Bill's concerned, selling things is such a *bore*.

At Georgian antiques you'll find the extraordinary Romain De Campe, bright red from decades of good food and better wine, looking like a human sunset. (If he sat in a bathful of iced water, there'd be an explosion of steam.) And surrounded by the tintinnabulation of time, the tickings and chimings of a hundred clocks, there's Michael Wiesel, so plump and bearded that he's Tweedledum to my 'dee. If we sat on a see-saw together, you'd have the visual expression of that irresistible force meeting its immovable object.

And let's not forget Fountain Frank, who can turn the most rusting pile of junk, or the inside of your grandmother's copper, or a marble caryatid from a fireplace into a passable Trevi. He's currently working on his apotheosis, fixing dancing dolphins to a succession of iron dishes so vast they might have come from a 16th century flying saucer. Hammering, welding, cursing, he'll soon have it ejaculating spendidly before some mansion in Armadale or Kew.

And if you drive up High Street, past the proliferating specialists in etchings, candle sticks and art nouveau, you'll find Gary Kay, immortalised as Rappaport in a novel by Morris Lurie. Gary, almost buried in the extravagance and absurdity of his Victoriana, muttering to himself like Captain Nemo in his Nautilus.

Yet for me the most interesting man in Australia's antique business is his near neighbour, the extraordinary and indeed *notorious* Graham Geddes. Geddes, whose shop is so stuffed with Roman torsos, Indian doorways, Spanish tables, Dutch chandeliers, French provincial farming implements and king-sized cast iron blackamoors that you need to smear yourself with Vaseline so that you can wriggle through the gaps. Here a Baroque bird cage, there Dr Caligari's cabinet, topped with a reliquary containing the tonsils of a saint, teetering over a blood-stained basket used beneath a revolutionary guillotine, amidst nomadic rugs hot from the humps of camels and old amphora still dripping Aegean sea water.

As you enter you're likely to find him indecently embracing

an ancient statue while shrieking the most inventive abuse at his quaking, frazzled staff. (Customers who've walked in on one of these arias of indecency have been known to reel white-faced from the shop.) Yet while he's always threatening them with the sack, just as they're forever threatening to resign, most of them remain loyal to the eccentric tyrant who so endlessly abuses them. It is, they seem to believe, his way of showing affection. In any case, after working for Graham Geddes even Atilla the Hun would be anticlimactic and boring.

Geddes reminds me of Joyce Carey's wonderful character Gully Jimson in *The Horse's Mouth*. Jimson was a crazed painter who would stand transfixed before an empty wall, any empty wall, and without asking anyone's permission would proceed to cover it with a raging mural. Graham has the same sort of fixed focus, the same indifference to compromise. His enthusiasms range from the merely fierce to the truly frightening and Saturday simply isn't Saturday unless I spend some time sitting with him in an office full of Buddhist bronzes, Aztec pottery dogs, Sotheby's catalogues, account books and photographs from his mysterious 'contacts' in Milan.

He's caught the Midnight Express in Turkey, discovered lost temples in the Burmese jungle, crashed Land Rovers on every continent and shocked the bejesus out of the Melbourne antique establishment by dramatically changing the taste of its customers.

Until the emotional drain became too great, Graham was a child psychologist. After a period running discos he, like St Joan hearing her voices, discovered antiques. But not for him the polite, highly polished stuff that passed for good taste. He'd dive into the flea and thieves' markets of France, explore the back streets of Madrid and persuade ageing Maharajahs to sell him everything from their elephant howdahs to their preposterous, bejewelled Rolls Royces.

Some years ago I introduced him to antiquities and now he has enough pieces of broken marble to refurbish the Forum. Indeed, when Graham lands at Athens airport the police throw a cordon around what's left of the Parthenon knowing that, in Geddes, they've someone in the Lord Elgin tradition who's capable of getting *anything* through Customs. Similarly the Pol Pot regime has issued Graham's photograph to tens of thousands of troops, lest he comes sniffing after Angkor Watt.

Graham is an expert in everything. In Chinese export porcelain. In the patination of old bronzes. In the crystalline structure of pentyllic marble. In the contra-posture of Roman statuary. He can approach a new field and, with his relentless enthusiasm, become well-informed in weeks. Where an academic may spend a lifetime studying the intricacies of attic vases, Graham has had to achieve the same insights overnight. (Otherwise the Mafiosi with whom one deals in a dozen countries will flog him fakes and he couldn't stand the humiliation.) The best Geddes stories are too libellous and scandalous for repetition and I'm sworn to secrecy. But what I can say is this — if you want it, Geddes either has it or will get it.

For example, if you were to mention that you'd visited the crypt of a monastery in Rome where the bones of dead monks were used for decoration (as indeed I have) and where you'd admired a very amusing chandelier made out of leg bones and rib cages, you'd have it dangling in your dining room in about a fortnight. Furthermore, Graham would be able to explain to you the subtleties of skeletal art, how the pelvis was employed differently after the 16th century.

Looking like a refugee from the lightweight division of World Championship Wrestling, Geddes's selling technique is as improbable as his stock. It can be summed up as 'take-it-or-leave-it-and-preferably-leave-it-and-if-you-don't-like-it-you-can-lump-it-because-I-didn't-want-to-sell-it-to-a-prick-like-you-in-the-first-place-so-why-don't-you-just-piss-off-and-get-out-of-my-shop'. He once threw, quite literally, one of Melbourne's most pompous knights through his front door. On another occasion, a customer was wrenching at a rush-upholstered ladder-back to test its strength, with the same vigour he'd been applying to the drawers of a rather delicate old dresser. Observing this vandalism from the vantage point of his office, Geddes left by another door and entered the shop posing as a customer. Whereupon he grabbed a second ladder-back and smashed it to pieces on the refectory table. This precipitated one of Graham's verbal barrages which produced a terrified 'you can't talk to me like that' response from the chap as he backed and stumbled his way to safety.

Graham's prices have a certain elasticity. If he dislikes you, they soar whereas they tumble (well, come down a little bit) if you're a friend. And he has the most devoted Who's Who clientele who seem to revel in his insults and tantrums. Indeed, you'll often see them brawling amongst themselves as they attempt to ply him with bank notes. And it's not an uncommon sight to see his customers swimming out in Port Phillip Bay towards the heads so that they can clamber aboard a cargo ship and have first claw at Geddes's latest container. Graham could sell them *anything* and, in due course, probably will.

Sitting at his desk all but buried in catalogues from Christie's, shrieking obscenities at anyone within earshot, Graham somehow exudes a sort of innocence and, more importantly, a remarkable enthusiasm for what he's doing. There's no doubt he performs a useful social service for the world-weary of Toorak, turning their boring money into fascination and prestige. Yet there's absolutely nothing cynical about Geddes — he enjoys what he does as much as anyone I've ever met, in any sphere of activity, anywhere on earth.

Call in next time you're passing. But for God's sake, don't wrench his ladder-back chairs or slam his drawers. And don't say you haven't been warned.

St Anthony's fire

Today's column has an 'R' certificate, a classification that contains a vulgar pun. I am dictating it sotto voce and will have it typed very quietly in the hope that it will escape the editor's attention. For it concerns the subject of flatus which, for some odd reason, has been overlooked by the *Age* during its hundred-odd years of publication. Yet let me hasten to add that what follows is in no way low-brow or sordid. It is, indeed, a scholarly treatise on a subject of fundamental importance.

A few weeks ago I visited a military museum outside Cairo — an enormous building that echoed, indeed *parodied* Versailles in its gilded interiors. Devoted to the bric-à-brac of brutality and the glories of revolution, it was packed with shells, cannon, uniforms and dioramas. Models of giant catapults and ram-headed battering rams. But undoubtedly the most entrancing display was a diorama labelled 'TURKIST FART, 18th CENTURY'. I studied it closely, unaware that bacteriological warfare or poison gas had been used in such early conflicts, only to discover that fart was a spelling error.

Nonetheless I was reminded of my most significant contribution to Australian television, the night I added 'fart' to its cathode vocabulary. While it was Kenneth Tynan who introduced *the* naughty word to British television, it was your columnist who first broke wind, as it were, on the ABC, in the course of my first appearance with Michael Parkinson. I cannot remember why I said it though I have the dim memory that I was trying to provoke the Rev. Fred Nile who'd protested my involvement in the International Year of the Child. But I distinctly remember an echoing intake of air from the studio audience and the way Mr Parkinson's eyes momentarily glazed.

(It recalled the time when an elephant defecated on the stage during the rehearsal of Aida and the conductor, Sir Thomas Beecham, laid down his baton and said: 'Terrible stage manners, but what a critic'.)

In the 17th century, breaking wind was known as St Anthony's Fire. I don't know whether the saint suffered from flatulence but, of course, it is not unknown among churchmen. As John Osborne reminded us in his three-act drama *Luther*, poor Martin was bedevilled with the problem and frequently punctuated his sermons with the most extraordinary abdominal detonations. As to the reference to fire, this reminds me that I once witnessed a remarkable demonstration of the fart's flammability, conducted by a man of the highest scientific and academic repute, a living legend at Melbourne University, in the lounge-room of Stephen Murray-Smith, famed editor of the literary journal *Overland*. It made you realise that human beings are really quite dangerous, particularly after certain meals. The Mel Brooks *Blazing Saddles* sequence in which a lot of bean-eating cowboys fired off a fusillade around the campfire should never be emulated for fear of producing a mushroom cloud.

Flatulence comes from the Latin *flatus* meaning blow or

breath. In Cockney slang, the terms beef heart, bullock's heart and dart all meant fart in the early 19th century but only raspberry (for tart) has survived. The phenomenon is lovingly recorded in one of the great limericks . . .

> There was a young man of La Plata
> Who was widely renowned as a farta
> His deafening reports at the Argentine sports
> Made him much in demand as a starta.

An English writer, Tom Newman, has done invaluable research into the topic discovering that flatulence was the ultimate disgrace in the Balkans and frequently punished by hanging. While Robert Graves's favourite emperor, the lovable Claudius, was distressed to learn that many of his subjects 'carried their respect for his imperial majesty to the point of perishing rather than farting in his presence'.

Given the problems of weightlessness in the cabin, and pressurisation in their space suits, NASA has had to provide astronauts with a fart-free diet. As satellites and such-like are steered in and out of orbit with little poofs from the rockets, I suppose unwanted blasts could cause changes in trajectory or even lead to one of those flaming re-entries. NASA has not released information on this special diet but one can safely assume that Heinz are has-beens.

This brings us to the place of the fart in art. Connoisseurs will be familiar with Aubrey Beardsley's illustration for *Lysistrata*. (Given that it rhymes with La Plata, there should be inspiration for another limerick.) But the great cultural application of flatulence was to be found in the theatre. I refer of course to the greatest star of the 1890s, Joseph Pujol Le Pétomane. Not even Sarah Bernhardt had his box-office appeal. Billing himself as 'the only one who pays no author's royalties', he'd take 20,000 francs in a single Sabbath performance. Tom Newman describes him wearing a red cap with black satin breeches specially tailored for the purpose. Apparently Joseph would begin with 'character farts, from the mason's round fart to the timid little fart of the young girl'. As his act 'knew no language barrier', this extraordinary soloist toured like Pavarotti, thunderous applause greeting his thunderous performances. He can claim to have farted before the crowned heads of Europe as, for one, King Leopold of the Belgians is known to have paid an incognito visit to a Parisian performance.

Arias, medleys, ballads — all were in the repertoire of this extraordinary artiste who had such astonishing control over his abdominal muscles. It is to be earnestly hoped that some young performer embraces this lost art and makes his or her debut on *New Faces* or Johnny Young's *Young Talent Time*.

Salvador Dali published an anonymous 19th century treatise entitled *The Art of Farting or the Sly Artilleryman's Manual*. The author, under the pseudonym of Count Trumpet, identified different modes of flatulence, and more recently J.P. Donleavy, author of *The Beastly Beatitudes of Balthazar B*, published an expurgated code on the topic. While I'm indebted to Tom Newman's researches (he discovered that, in the 15th century 'prostitutes crossing the toll bridge at Montluc could pay their way either with four deniers or a fart'), I am more deeply indebted to one of my regular correspondents, whom I customarily address as H.J.S. of Tasmania. H.J. was very senior in that state's judiciary. Now in his eighties, he writes to me each week, regaling me with elegantly expressed anecdotes from the court rooms. Rumpole of the Bailey comes a bad third to H.J.S. of Tasmania.

I quote from his latest . . . 'As to Le Pétomane, I'm ashamed that I (ignorant bum!) have never heard of him. Is he a real person or a compatriate of Robinson Crusoe and Lemuel Gulliver? One is familiar with these fictitious figures of literary history who have become more real than their creators but with the moderns it is more difficult. I am never quite sure whether Barry Humphries really exists or whether he is merely the brainchild of Dame Edna Everage. But Le Pétomane's prowess reminds me of an old doggerel description of a great farting contest. It is rather vulgar (as I hope our exchanges are not!) so I do not quote it except for the final couplet which I feel redeems it.

'After wading through the details of the contest and the deeds and mishaps of the contestants the doggerelist (good word?) describes the impeccable behaviour of the winner after the judges have announced her success in the said competition "amid shouts of applause". (Which incidentally he makes to rhyme with drawers.) The final couplet is . . .

>So she turned to the crowd as they started to sing
>And farted the first verse of God Save the King.

'That it should be recognisable as the *first* verse is surely a challenge to Le Pétomane.

'On the general subject of Farting, I would like to see a revival of the old and to me more aesthetically pleasing spelling "faht" which, in my youth, was always used by persons of refinement when writing of the action. This was only discarded because of the confusion (with the new-fangled habit of abbreviations) with Fahrenheit in our measurement of temperature. This objection is no longer valid since our adoption of the Celsiarse scale. My favoured spelling seems essentially logical. A well-delivered and comforting faht partakes far more of the soft aspiration of an "h" than the roughness of an "r".'

Nicely put, H.J. And a splendid note to end on, as the actress said to the bishop.

King Cheops's royal ship

Just before noon on the 26 May 1954 Kamal el-Mallakh, a young Egyptian, made one of the major archaeological discoveries of all time. Yet his name was excluded from the official history. Just as one pharaoh might obliterate the cartouche (i.e. royal signature) of his predecessor from statues and obelisks, an attempt was made to remove Kamal's signature from this most remarkable achievement. It's as if Howard Carter's name had been expunged from the saga of Tutenkhamen.

Kamal is now the arts editor of al-Ahram, *Cairo's most powerful daily paper. And a few days ago I sat in the office of this affable, formidable man who needed little encouragement to retell his story...*

Meetings in my office, in most western offices, are forever interrupted by the electric intrusions of the telephone. Not so in Cairo where, in every official's office, there's an endless stream of *human* interruptions. Kamal fobs off a lengthening queue of supplicants and subordinates with gestures or cups of Turkish coffee, for nothing is going to stop his narrative. Some give up, murmur 'Maalesh' (which translates to something between *c'est la vie* and what the hell) and shuffle off, while others eavesdrop.

'I began my career as an illustrator of the books of our great men and thinkers. I'm talking of men who died generations ago. I was also a student of architecture, a lecturer in an arts faculty wanting to do my Masters when a new Dean was appointed, the son of someone very well connected to the Farouk entourage. He knew very little about the subjects and I found it humiliating. So I refused to submit. You see, I've always been very stubborn.'

(A well-known poet sitting on the couch beside us smiles in agreement, echoing 'very'.)

'My days were numbered, but a new Minister for Education was appointed, one of the greatest men in our country. He was one of many children in a very, very poor family in one of the poorest of villages. He'd been born partly sighted and when he was five his parents took him to the local barber who said he could restore his vision. Needless to say, he completely blinded him. Yet he went on to become a great scholar, travelling to France and marrying a graduate from the Sorbonne. They've just made a film of his life called *Escape from Shadows*.

'Well, this wonderful man took me aside and said "Kamal, I want you to hide in the Antiquities Department for a while, until things get better for you." I protested that I was uninterested in antiquities, that I was an artist and an architect. He said we must Egyptianise the control of our heritage, instead of letting the foreigners tell us what to do. "I want you to take this appointment and, if after three months you're unhappy, you may complete your Masters." So although I knew nothing and cared nothing for all that old rubble, I agreed. And the Minister arranged for me to be taught, every day, by one of our most knowledgeable archaeologists.

'Three months later he rang and asked whether I wanted to return to my old career and I said "Certainly not", for I was fascinated and wholly committed to the new job. Studying the architecture, the religion, the hieroglyphs, I was beginning to understand some of the complexities of the past.

'I was attached to the staff of an ageing archaeologist who wandered the country from Luxor to Nubia, and when he unexpectedly died, they gave me his job. I was only twenty-three. Shortly thereafter the very cultured and knowledgeable Frenchman who was the head of our Antiquities Department and a close friend of Farouk's, was forced to leave Egypt because of our revolution. He was replaced by someone whose father was close to the junta, whose archaeological credentials were, to say the least, unimpressive.

'By now I was in charge of the whole pyramids area, doing some of the first restoration work on the sphinx. There were, as you know, a number of pits near the pyramid, in alignment with its sides. There were theories that they'd once contained boats for ceremonial or religious usage, although there was no solid evidence. One of them was open, gradually filling with rubbish, and another had been used in Ptolemaic times for tombs.

'I felt sure there had to be another pit or two, still undiscovered. But then, people had been walking around the pyramids for 5,000 years and none had been discovered. So I kept my thoughts to myself.

'Then I got an opportunity to do something. A child had fallen into the open pit and was hurt. I went to the new director and said "We must do something about that pit", and he agreed. He gave me £200 as a budget. No, not very much. But it turned out to be a very spectacular investment.

'In the course of fixing the pit in which the child had fallen, I found almost microscopic traces of cedar wood. Added to the hieroglyphic evidence, I was convinced that ceremonial boats *had* been provided for Cheops. As you know, the pyramids are aligned to the sun and involve the worship of Ra, the sun god.

'On the side of the pyramid where I expected the pits might be, we unearthed a rather crooked fence which everyone assumed had been built there much, much later. Perhaps 1,000 years later. It was made up of detritus of the construction, from fragments of granite and basalt. Just the leftovers. The fact that it was poorly constructed and ran at a strange angle to the pyramid was not consistent, of course, with the formality of the Old Kingdom. Yet it seemed to me to be truly ancient, to date from Cheops. Therefore, might it not be camouflage? A crooked fence to hide the pits beneath?

'I used to carry a long iron spike to kill scorpions and snakes, though I was later to find that the human being was far, far more dangerous. Poking around with my stick I found an ancient layer of mud (more camouflage?) and, poking deeper, came up with white stone on the tip! Good quality limestone. Others suggested that the stone was merely a foundation for the fence but, as you know, Egyptian architects did not use foundations. Not even the great Pyramid itself, which weighs so many millions of tons, has foundations. It simply sits on the plateau. So I began to poke around with my stick until I found a trace of coloured gypsum — the pink mortar cement of the Old

Kingdom. My stick had gone *between* two buried stones!

'Now I was convinced that I was close to discovery. I walked up and down poking with the stick until I'd outlined the entire pit. And not just one pit, but *two* pits.

'I *knew* I had discovered my solar boats.

'I had my workmen clear two massive limestone blocks, huge and beautifully shaped. The ancient Egyptians had been working in stone since the step pyramid of King Zoser in the third dynasty. Now, a hundred years later, they were masterful in their craftsmanship. Shaping stones with the simplest tools, moving giant blocks without the wheel, without the pulley, with only the lever and human strength.

'As we cleared away the old fence and the camouflage of mud, we found two sets of stones, 40 to the west, 41 to the east. Precisely along the axis of the south face of the pyramid. And on one of the blocks I read the cartouche of King Djedefre, the son of Cheops.

'I felt it proper to go back to my new boss and tell him that we may have made a major discovery. But he dismissed what I had to say. Who do you think you are? Howard Carter? "No, he was an illustrator from the Metropolitan Museum in New York and I am an Egyptian archaeologist", I said boastfully. He told me that I was being silly nonetheless. If there was a boat down there, white ants would long since have destroyed it. Instead he asked me where he could get a statue of Rameses II to put in the square outside the railway station. I told him where there were one or two gigantic Rameses and how to arrange to have one transported. Now, will you come? No, he was too busy.

'So I went back to the pyramid and had a hole hacked very carefully through the limestone, just big enough to lower my body in. Now I was in the position of a clown, head down, feet in the air. But the blocks are almost 6 ft deep, and I'm a little over 6 ft. And there I was, dangling upside down, staring into the darkness. It was midday and my eyes were dazzled, and I could see nothing.

'But I could *smell* something. The smell of cedar and of balsam. I smelt incense, a very holy, holy smell. I smelt time, centuries. I smelt history. It was the most wonderful smell which, sadly, disappeared after three weeks. When we open the other pit, scientists must analyse that smell because it's so fantastic. But still I couldn't see because of the glare. So like a cat I closed my eyes for a while, and then reopened them in the gloom.

'I could still see nothing, because of the powdered limestone that had floated down. But now I *knew* I was right, that I'd found the boat.

'I used my shaving mirror to reflect the beam of sunlight — the light of Ra, the sun-god, into the pit. And it fell upon the shape of an oar. And there, stacked neatly, in row after row, were the dismantled pieces of the boat of the king.

'I kissed the ground and thanked god — Ra — and went back to Cairo and told the director. He came out and looked and his face went white. "But this is the most important discovery, even more important than Tutenkhamen." "Well", I said modestly and calmly, "it's 2,500 years older." Yes, I was icy calm.

'I'd been worried that the oxygen rushing into the tomb might destroy the wood, turn it into dust. But when I saw the condition of the wood with the light from my shaving mirror, I knew it would be all right. The ropes, the straw matting, everything was beautifully preserved. Because the tomb had been sealed so tight, hermetically. And the humidity and the temperature had been stable for almost 5,000 years.

'Almost immediately, I began to lose control of my boat. I was accused of vanity but, had I been vain, I'd have opened the second pit immediately. But no, I left that for others, at some future time, when we knew about conservation techniques. You see, there were factions in the Antiquities Department between the archaeologists who believed *they* were practising the most important of the sciences (because it involves our most ancient history) and the architects who tended to have the big workforces and the bigger budgets. Being both an archaeologist *and* an architect, I was acceptable to neither faction. I was caught beneath them. It was like being crushed under a granite block.

'So once again my life was swinging between the good and the bad, the bad and the good.

'This young man', (and Kamal pointed to a rather elderly gentleman in the ever-growing queue of people waiting to see him), 'well, this *old* man as he's now become, was with me at the beginning. It was he who found a way to introduce electric light into the tomb — through a little pipe. At first we thought it was for ventilation, but later realised it was for the soul of the king to enter and leave.

'Did I tell you that every piece of the boat — well over 1,000 — was individually numbered like a child's toy kit? These days it would be so easy to put it together with a computer. But then, of course, Egypt had no computers. So it had to be done by hand, piece by piece. Which is why it took twenty long years.

'Of course I'm obstinate and opinionated and all the rest. You have to be. Archaeologists, like Carter, have to be totally sure of themselves. The odds against you when you're working in the sand in the desert and the sun are simply enormous. There's little hope of finding anything. You must be *convinced* that you are right. You are so dwarfed by the magnitude and age of ancient Egypt that it all but crushes your individuality. You must fight back against this and all the opposition. So I have always fought, and will, I hope, always fight.'

I have waited half my life to see King Cheops's royal ship but nothing prepared me for its beauty. The oldest boat on the planet is also the loveliest. You stand beneath a gigantic, curving shape that reminds you of the Vikings' craft or the gondola of Venice, yet neither have a smidgin of its grace. I was reminded of standing beneath the Anglo-French *Concorde* for the boat has something of its purity and sense of purpose.

Made from the cedars of Lebanon, still faintly perfumed, the ship is over 43 metres long and 5.9 metres in the beam. It seems more appropriate to flight than to floating.

Kamal calls his discovery the Solar Bark, and believes it was destined to carry the dead king of Egypt in his eternal round across the sky with the Sun God. Others believe it was a funerary barge, to carry Cheops's embalmed body down the Nile from Memphis, his capital, to Giza for his burial. Others believe that Cheops actually used the boat for pilgrimages to the most sacred sites along the Nile. Whatever its purpose, it is the most breathtaking object I've ever seen.

The fourth dynasty was the apotheosis of style and elegance in ancient Egypt. Though pharaohs were to rule for thousands more years, the culture would never again achieve the same refinement.

In its shape, it evokes the curve of the simple papyrus boat, the craft made by the ancient Egyptians (and still made in the delta today) by binding papyrus together. And the papyrus was also the inspiration for the subtle columns that surround the king's cabin and the captain's 'bridge'.

I've yet to see a photograph that *begins* to do it justice. However there's a fine sequence of photographs by John Ross in *The Boat Beneath the Pyramid* published by Thames and Hudson.

In contrast to Cheops's pyramid, Cheops's boat is alive. It is as remarkable in its delicacy as the pyramid is in its massive stolidity. The boat speaks to us of air, of water, of humanity — where the pyramid remains implacably silent, a chip off the block of eternity.

It's an irony that the only image that remains of Cheops, the man who built the boat *and* the world's mightiest and most famous monument, survives. It's a tiny, smudged little ivory the size of your thumb.

The problem of war begins with hatred

Twenty years ago Stanley Kramer made a movie in Melbourne about the Third World War. Now *On the Beach* is a piece of nostalgia, a costume drama. The city it depicted *has* been destroyed, but by property developers rather than nuclear weapons. To some extent, that symbolises the success of MAD, the acronym for Mutually Assured Destruction, the basis of 'the balance of terror' between Kremlin and Pentagon. But with every passing hour the chance of war through misunderstanding or misadventure grows.

There are over 17,000 nuclear war heads in the Great Powers' armoury. Is it possible to disarm them? Can man, at this stage, undiscover fire? And can he do so without burning his fingers?

The problem of war begins with hatred. Brecht said 'Even hatred of violence distorts a man's features.' While, in a sentence reminiscent of Jesus Christ, Jean Paul Sartre observed 'It is enough that one man hate enough for hate to gain, little by little, all mankind.' Hatred is, if you like, a form of fission that produces an uncontrollable chain reaction.

To me, as a Humanist, the most admirable aspect of Christian theology is its plea for universal love. How tragic that Christianity persistently ignores its messiah's most intelligent commandment. Like Sartre, I see World War III as a macrocosm of the hostilities and prejudices that pollute and destroy our personal relations.

It is very hard to hate an individual human being. What you must do is to turn him into an abstraction by affixing a label. It is the labels we fear and hate. America is full of people who are willing to jeopardise the survival of life on this planet because they hate the label of communism. Yet not one in a million of them has ever met a communist.

I suppose that hatred has been a useful human emotion, that without it we might still be languishing in the primal brine. It is probably an essential evolutionary tool, to sharpen our wits and get the adrenalin pumping so that we could cope with sabre-tooth tigers and sundry predators. But when you give haters nuclear weapons, the emotion becomes the most dangerous of anachronisms.

We're used to hostility between the Judaic, Islamic and Christian worlds who institutionalise hatreds, historic hatreds, fixed colours on the ever-changing Rubik's Cube of changing alliances. But who could have expected the overnight enmity between Britain and Argentina? There might have been a few punch-ups at soccer matches, but suddenly they were ready to obliterate each other.

The differences between human beings are so very marginal. A few centimetres in height, a few kilos in weight, a few degrees in religious longitude or intellectual latitude, some pigmentation of the skin. Some slight variations in sexuality or in ideology. Step back a bit and the differences are so slight as to be infinitesimal, invisible. Yet to human beings these differences are the stuff of prejudices that lead to holocausts. We are, quite literally, our own worst enemies. Having triumphed over the other life forms, we can juggle with our environment and chromosomes. Yet we cannot cope with variations on the human theme.

Sometimes it seems the smaller the difference, the greater the hatred. Certainly that seems to be the case in Northern Ireland between Christians who worship the same God, and sing much the same hymns in the same brogues. Yet the divisions between them have filled a hundred graveyards. And, believe it or not, the Catholic deaf use a different sign language to the Protestant deaf.

You know, we can have everything in common. We can be of the same race, religion, sex, class and political persuasion and *still* find things to divide us. That's why the most intense hatreds are not *between* political parties, but within them.

If you're an American, think how wonderfully easy it is to hate a Russian. First of all, there's that word: Russian. In itself, such a splendid abstraction. Then there are terms like Communist and Marxist which rate with werewolf and vampire on the goose-bump list. And we mustn't forget Atheist, in some way the most alarming abstraction of all. And when you pile them all up — Russian, Red, Communist, Marxist, Atheist — you're orchestrating conditioned responses augmented by the profoundest of ignorance.

The fact that ordinary Russians have almost identical appetites to Americans, share the same lust for cars and washing machines, high calorie foods and ice creams, and would probably kill for a McDonald's hamburger, is irrelevant. Not only irrelevant, but unknown.

Winston Churchill's Iron Curtain has been a very useful barrier for American ideologues because it has placed a communications gulf between two worlds with too much in common. (A mere trickle of Americans visit the Soviet, less than 100,000 a year or one day's intake at Disneyland.)

So it's very easy for the Christian fundamentalists, the born-again yahoos of the Moral Majority who helped get Reagan into the White House to depict the Soviet (and there's another of those frightening buzz words) as dark and satanic. Mind you, they do get a little confused in their iconography.

The other night I heard the Rev. Jerry Falwell, that theological used car salesman, suggest that American immorality might be punished by God employing an apocalyptic hail of Russian missiles. This would seem to suggest that Soviet Russia is God's instrument for improving the morality of America. Yet Rev. Falwell also sees America's missiles and American A-bombs as serving God's purpose, in punishing those godless atheists. Mind you, it's the sort of inconsistency you'd expect from a man and a movement who profess belief in a 6,000-year-old world and a seven-day creation while, in the same breath, employing computer technology to pick the pockets of their gullible congregations.

Of course, the same manipulations of ignorance are employed by the Kremlin, and are *essential* to their purpose. To visit Russia is to see how grotesquely images of the USA are distorted by the regime. America is the most paradoxical of societies, offering the best and worst in education, medicine, cinema, science, literature and social justice. But just as the Soviet is represented as little else than the land of labour camps and lubiankas, America is characterised as a nation of Jim Crow lynchings and imperialism. In each case, a giant pot calls the kettle black. Meanwhile the rest of the world looks on in sorrow and terror at these gross and grotesque over-simplifications, at the half-truths each side uses to justify its imperialism, its manipulation of minor powers and its nuclear posturing.

In many ways the two societies are too alike. In both we have elites who profit, in one way and another, from such paranoia. Whose power and prestige are largely or even totally dependent on this histrionic huffing and puffing, on being able to postulate that the other side, the enemy, is both insatiable and unspeakably evil.

Mind you, I cannot believe that there are people around Brezhnev who are quite as crazy as some of Reagan's recruits. We have the extraordinary behaviour of James Watt who's turning over America's national parks to the miners and drillers and timber cutters, who argues that the Second Coming of Christ is so imminent that it doesn't really matter what we do with a planet that will soon be theologically redundant. God forbid that the same attitudes permeate the Pentagon for clearly born-again Christians should *not* be in control of nuclear weapons any more than ayatollahs or Libyan loonies.

And yet Thomas Jones, a deputy under-secretary of the Defence Department, believes that Russia could rebuild its industry after a nuclear war 'in two to four years', that the US could do the same if it wanted. Indeed, if Americans wish to survive a nuclear attack, all they need to do is 'dig a hole, cover it with a couple of doors and then throw a metre of dirt on top. It's the dirt that does it.'

A former Boeing officer and Defence Department official in past Republican administrations, Jones believes that the US could almost benefit from a nuclear war. 'We can get recovery time down to where we can start production in something like four to twelve weeks and be back at present levels of production in one year', he says, stressing that a Third World War will do less damage than a reasonably long recession. 'Everybody is going to make it', says Mr Jones, 'if there are enough shovels to go around.'

Passing quickly over the possibility of accidental nuclear war (and in 1975, 1976 and 1977 alone over 15,000 military personnel were removed from access to nuclear weapons when it was found they were drunks, drug addicts or otherwise mentally deranged) we return to a world where Russia and America echo and re-echo each other's assumptions and rhetoric. While both societies profess a commitment to freedom, the independence of the weaker nations, to the desire of peace, both do their dirty deals, sully their ideals and beat their plough shares into swords. United Nations Charters and Helsinki Accords aren't worth the paper they're written on — or the blood they've been written in.

There's not much that can be done about these two super powers, those monsters locked in their dance of death. If one side or the other says that they will stop making this missile or withdraw that weapon from their armoury, it's because that missile is redundant or that weapon has lost its strategic relevance. Hardly a week goes by without some piece of empty posturing by Brezhnev or Reagan which we, in our fearful gullibility, leap upon as some sign of hope. When in fact they're trying to cheat each other at nuclear poker.

So it's great for the emotions to speak about peace with transcendental fervour. To demand instant unilateral disarmament is, on one level, the most profound piece of commonsense but on another, it's an absurdity, like asking for eternal life. Like international disarmament, eternal life has much to recommend it but it's very, very hard to achieve.

I've no doubt that we can place growing pressure on the USA through the swelling ranks of the Peace Movement. But how can we place similar pressures on the Soviet, on a society where to be dissident is to be classified as insane, to invite a life sentence in the political prison thinly disguised as a psychiatric ward? There was hope, for a while, that the Poles would start to break down the Soviet monolith, a hope that was cruelly and tragically dashed.

I suppose our best hope is that the middle ranking powers who can see both the Soviet and the US more rationally, more clearly, can exercise a variety of pressures upon them. Economic, political, cultural. Perhaps the emerging power of China can continue to undermine the silliness of bipolar policies.

And there's another danger. As a member of the Communist Party in the 1950s I remember laughing at Bertrand Russell suggesting that the Third World War would be between Russia and China. Surely the old bloke had gone senile as it was an article of faith that war was impossible between socialist states. Well, Bert saw the future more clearly than we did and a China-Soviet conflict is by no means an improbability. Indeed, when I was last in Moscow Soviet paranoia about the USA was comparatively muted while Muscovites prepared for war with their erstwhile comrades in Peking.

There is one area in which the American people are far more ignorant than their Russian counterparts. And that is, of course, in their experience of war. To stand in Leningrad in a cemetery filled with more than a million dead is to remember the long historic sufferings of the Russian people in foreign invasions. It is to understand their enduring fear of a resurgent Germany, their historic desire for a buffer zone between them and an historic enemy. Whatever's going on in the Kremlin, I believe that the Russian people have absolutely no war-like fantasies because they've experienced the realities of war.

In contrast, war for most Americans is something that happens in the movies or on television, a long, long way away. Just as we find it hard to conceive of personal death, I believe that Americans find it hard to conceive of the reality of war as it has, thus far, been an export industry.

There is, of course, no moral difference between the fire bombing of Dresden and the nuclear bombing of Hiroshima. The victims were just as dead. The qualitative difference is simply radioactivity, the punitive clause that will keep punishing the survivors until, as has been said, they may envy the dead. Indeed, it may be that world war becomes more likely if and when the nuclear mushrooms fade away. Somehow there's still some hope in a conventional war, no matter how unconventional the weapons may be — and the non-nuclear armoury includes poison gases and 'biological weapons'. In contrast there is no hope with nuclear weapons.

But what chance do we have of ridding ourselves of this pestilence simply by singing folk songs, chanting slogans and saying rude things about Ronnie Raygun? If we were able to force unilateral disarmament on the West, in some unimaginable set of circumstances, we'd be surrendering to a system that blasphemes against its ideals and that has proved itself quite capable of vindicating the worst slanders of the American Right.

I suppose if it comes to the choice of being dead or red, I'll choose red every time. For Soviet-style communism will prove to be a passing phenomena, however long it lasts. Even if it lasted as long as the Egyptian dynasties, that's a mere 3,000 years. Whereas death, as those road safety commercials used to remind us thirty years ago, is so permanent. In other words, we could be confident that humans would rise up against communism whereas, despite Christian allegations to the contrary, there's not much evidence that they can rise up from the grave. But though I'd rather be red than dead, there are millions who, it would seem, prefer the crypt to the Kremlin.

So we return to the problem. Everyone agrees that nuclear weapons are nasty and unpleasant. But how to get rid of them? How do we get the genii back in the bottle?

At this stage of the Cold War, at this stage of what has already been the most destructive century in human history, it's no time for platitudes or self-deception. Of course we need to develop an oceanic, global consciousness of the value of human, of all life. Of course we need to sing our songs and march our marches. But it's not enough to hate President Reagan. In fact, there's not much point in hating at all. Because as that well-known Marxist Jesus Christ once said (or was it that well-known Christian Jean Paul Sartre?) hatred is where the whole problem begins.

My heart goes out to Her Royal Maj

'Christine was astonished to see how deeply in love her husband seemed to be with the Queen.' The *Sun*

As an ardent monarchist (I did but see her passing by and yet I'll love her till I die) my heart goes out to Her Royal Maj. I think it's *terrible* the way Fleet and Downing Streets have been making cheap jokes about the man who sat on her bed. And it's awful the way we've been allowed to invade her privacy, to read the innermost details of her private life. Why can't the poor Queen be left in peace to have a squalid love affair, if that's what she wants?

Obviously they'd been seeing each other regularly for some time now. Then, suddenly, they're sprung in the royal boudoir by some sanctimonious spoilsport. Some forelock-tugging Uriah Heep who rushed off and dobbed her into the Duke. Whereupon Whitehall decided to construct a Big Lie so as to avoid diplomatic damage. After all, everything had been going so well for the Brits. Lady Di winning hearts, the armed services winning the war and *Chariots of Fire* winning the Oscar. No thought was given to the Queen's feelings; the emotional needs and appetites of the woman are brushed aside and the propaganda machine goes into high gear fabricating a palpably absurd story about an intruder.

They must reckon we all came down in the last shower. A working class yobbo climbing over the fence at least a dozen times, wandering through the labyrinth of the palace undetected and happening, *just happening*, to come upon the Queen's bedroom. Pull the other one — it whistles 'Rule Britannia'.

It's perfectly obvious what really happened. The Queen had organised some drugged cocoa for the sentries and given the chap a diagram, hastily sketched on the back of a court circular.

'God save our gracious queen', we all chorus, adding the bit about sending her victorious, happy and glorious. Well, she may be victorious and glorious, but any fool can see she's not happy. Particularly when the Duke has slept in a separate bedroom either down the hall or down the stairs, depending on which newspaper you believe, since 1949. In any case, you could tell the marriage was in trouble by the way he's been walking further and further behind her in recent years. Clearly the woman's had a desperate need for male companionship, except where can she get it? That is, really *male* companionship. As *Brideshead* reminds us, the overwhelming majority of the English upper class are not heterosexually inclined but prefer to have sleazy affairs with the working class. 'Rough trade', they call it.

So in her desperation she sees the glowing face of an ardent royalist, cheering as she rides by in one of her gilded juggernauts. She makes discreet enquiries through a trusted maid and thus begins a harmless even poignant dalliance.

And why not? After all, it's a palace tradition. Ever since that princess had it off with a frog, your royals have been drawn to the virility of the lower orders. In *Henry VIII* Shakespeare makes mention of the king's promiscuity with 'a little touch of Harry in the night' while a few coronations later we had Charles II lusting after Nell Gwyn. There was Louis XIV and Madame Pompadour, Edward VII and Lily Langtree, Hamlet and Ophelia, the Prince of Wales and Mrs Fitzherbert — even Prince Charming and Cinderella.

Come to think of it, there is something of the Cinderella story in this latest account of star-crossed lovers. Except that instead of leaving behind a glass slipper, Mr Fagan would have left behind a glass syringe as, apparently, he was a heroin addict.

But to return to my theme of the loneliness of queendom. You'll recall the nursery rhyme about the king in his counting house counting out his money while the poor queen was in the parlour, consoling herself with bread and honey. This sort of desolation found new expression in the life of Queen Victoria after the death of her consort when she turned to her live-in yobbo, the magnificently sporran'd John Brown. Her son, the Prince of Wales, had more affairs than you've had hot breakfasts, with a season's ticket at most of London's lowest dives. And Elizabeth's dad only got to be king because his brother got the hots for some American sexpot.

So whether it's the Tsarina with Rasputin or Princess Anne with Mark Phillips or Elizabeth I with Robert Cecil and Walter Raleigh, your royal personages have been drawn to the ignoble like moths to the lamp, finding in the working class a virility and vitality that is so sadly lacking amongst the effete, inbred aristocracy. Indeed, it may be the way the British royal family revitalises itself. Without discreet transfusions of lower-class corpuscles, they'd all have become silly as wheels, like George III.

No one complains when Prince Andrew, known far and wide as Randy Andy, goes slumming in the least salubrious of night spots. No one objected when Prince Charles went out on the tiles. Even Princess Margaret was allowed to marry a member of the paparazzi, Tony 'flash bulb' Snowdon.

There's a famous quote from a British matron watching Sarah Bernhardt play Cleopatra. 'How different, how very different from the home life of our own dear queen!' But why shouldn't the queen have a bit of fun? I mean, she spends most of her life dragging around laying foundation stones and listening to that appalling jingle, the National Anthem. (Which reminds one of the time her Mum heard it being played on television during the Cup final and said 'Oh, do turn it off, it's so embarrassing unless one is there — like hearing the Lord's Prayer when playing canasta.')

If anyone deserves the solace of romance, it's Elizabeth II. Yet the only declaration of love she's had in the last twenty years was that 'I did but see her passing by' line from an old age pensioner who happened to be Prime Minister of Australia.

Some years ago it was revealed that the Queen's favourite television programme was *Kojak* (I put this down to the Royal Family's obsession with bald-headed men, as shown in their enthusiasm for that awful Winston Churchill). Thinking back, it's quite clear that she was tiring of the fops, dandies and quiche-eaters around her and yearning for a real man. Well, now that she's found one it behoves us to do the decent thing and let them alone.

Good on her, that's what I say. I think it's great she's found someone and I hope to goodness they haven't been frightened off by all the publicity. But if they have stepped up the security in the palace grounds she could always hire that royal look-alike who does supermarket openings. Using her as a stand-in, Elizabeth could sneak out the back door for assignations in Fagan's bed-sitter. That's the one good thing about the Queen — she dresses so appallingly that she'd pass for an ordinary housewife just about anywhere. If she whizzed down to the pantry and stuffed a stick of celery and a packet of Omo in a string bag, she'd be rendered invisible.

On *Gallipoli*

In the imaginary menagerie of childhood we have three wise monkeys to warn us about gossip, three little pigs to warn us about sloppy building codes and an elephant with six blind men to warn us about film critics.

You'll remember the scene. Each of the blind men takes

hold of a different part of the mammoth and comes to a different conclusion. The one who grabs its tail says 'How like a stick!' The one who fondles its trunk says 'How like a hose', whilst the one who embraces a leg says 'How like a tree!' Everybody, therefore, is in disagreement. Yet everyone has part of the truth.

So when I applaud *Gallipoli* as being a splendid film — and Bob Ellis leads a counter-attack in which he damns it as one of the worst films ever made, it's just possible that both of us are right.

For the significance in a film lies, finally, in the refractive views we can take of it. If it has any sort of complexity, a dozen people may react to it in a dozen different yet legitimate ways.

Colin Bennett was a fine critic and yet walked out on one of my favourite films, Walerian Borowczyk's *Gotto, Island of Love*. I remember we sat in a restaurant afterwards and yelled at each other about it. If one of my most admired US films, Kazan's *America America!* ever got an enthusiastic review, I must have missed it. And it seems that only India's Satyajit Ray shares my belief that Mark Donskoi's *Gorky Trilogy* represents the zenith of Soviet cinema. I've read acres of accolades for *Apocalypse Now*, a film I regard as a high-camp, racist travesty. While many people whose judgment I admire rejoiced in *Mad Max I*, I saw it as one of the most malign, manipulative pieces of moviemaking since Leni Riefenstahl made *Victory of Faith* for Hitler. Woody Allen's *Stardust Memories* was reviled by every significant New York critic, yet I'm convinced it's Allen's finest work.

But in believing that I'm right, I'm not saying that everybody else is wrong.

In film, as in everything, there are as many views as viewpoints. Indeed, one's own reaction to a film can be profoundly different on a second or third viewing — as was the case for me with Visconti's *Death in Venice*. The first time I found it insufferably twee and pretentious. A few nights back, on television, I was fascinated by its austerity, elegance and passion.

A confession. For many years I was that lowest of the low, that literary leper, a critic. A Tiberius of the typewriter, butchering other people's efforts in television, film and theatre with a blood-stained Olivetti. Then, suddenly, I saw the error of my ways. No more hacking off heads for my trophy room. Never again would I destroy the work of years or a lifetime in a single, careless paragraph.

So these days I write about film only when, it seems to me, everyone has missed the point. For example, exasperated by reviews both here and overseas which had *Picnic at Hanging Rock* based on real events, I set out to explain the metaphysics of the mystery, showing that the film was not some misty documentary but a piece of science fiction, a sort of Space Odyssey in petticoats. It's true that a friendship with Joan and Daryl Lindsay gave me a number of clues to *Picnic*, to Joan's obsession with time. But even a superficial reading of the text should have been enough to clarify the story's secret. (See 'Into another dimension', *The Unspeakable Adams*, page 63.)

And in the continuing debate on *Gallipoli*, critics and audiences missed the central point revealed in this column some months ago. That the film is not so much about war as the homosexual dimension in Australian mateship. In any male friendship, for that matter. In my view the young runners could have been off to compete in the Olympics (as they were in *Chariots of Fire*) rather than heading for death in the Dardanelles. Whilst hardly Oscar and Bosey (our heroes may not have known what 'homosexual' meant), it was clear that they were having an intense love affair. After my column appeared David Williamson rang and said, yes, that's exactly what they were trying to do. Halfway through the scripting, he and Peter had realised that they were telling a homosexual love story.

Now I'd go further and say that the film is, quite specifically but perhaps unconsciously, about the relationship between David and Peter themselves. The young, innocent blond soldier is a narcissistic self-image of Peter whilst the darker, more sardonic character is a reflection of David. I'm not suggesting that these two happily married heterosexuals will be seen haunting gay bars — simply that they have made a film which explores the emotions kindled in the act of collaboration.

Of all the attacks on *Gallipoli*, the angriest came from Bob Ellis who saw it as a limp-wristed travesty. But in his response Bob was, I suspect, as jealous of the relationship between Williamson and Weir as he was of the film's success. For Ellis's well-known obsession with Williamson clearly has a homoerotic dimension. Bob has said as much in earlier writings, in the old *Nation Review*.

Meanwhile the world's critics, Bob Ellis amongst them, have entirely missed the point of David Puttnam's film *Chariots of Fire*. I wrote a review of the film months ago, in the form of a personal letter to David, which produced a response of 'You're right, of course, you bastard'. I make it public now because of impatience with so many blind men groping at that cinematic elephant.

Like *Gallipoli*, and so many other works of art, *Chariots* is a self-portrait. This time, both characters are refractions, or aspects, of a single man. The producer, David Puttnam himself. You may remember a column I wrote describing a dinner with Lord Grade and Puttnam where Lew told us that God was his executive producer. Grade gave us instance after instance where the Almighty had intervened in his career (I wonder if that includes introducing him to Robert Holmes à Court?) thus making him the most powerful of Britain's media moguls. At the end of this improbable revelation, Puttnam said that he, too, was protected and directed by the Almighty. God, insisted David, had taken a personal interest in everything he'd done — so much so that He really deserved a credit in *Midnight Express*. At first we laughed at David's comments, thinking he was lampooning Lew's. Not so. David was in deadly earnest.

Little wonder that I began smiling in the dark almost as soon as *Chariots* started. You have two runners striving for excellence, for victory. One of them is a Christian missionary who is, in effect, running for Jesus. The other is a Jew who is running from anger and ambition, so that he can throw his success in the teeth of the anti-semites.

49

We are being presented with the mixed emotions of David Puttnam in his struggle to become the most prominent British producer since Sir Michael Balcon. On the one hand, David, the moralist, makes films for Jesus. On the other, he makes them for personal ambition, for such secular rewards as money, acclaim and power. Like most interesting men and women, Puttnam seethes with contradictions. So while *Chariots* might seem to be about British spunk, it's really about those contradictions. A portrait of a man who feels he may be a Jeckyll and Hyde.

(I don't remember any critic looking at Barry McKenzie and seeing, as they should have, a distorted self-portrait of its creator, Barry Humphries, full of his horrors about sexuality and alcohol.)

Oddly enough, Bob Ellis regarded *Chariots of Fire* as one of the finest films ever made and wrote a tribute to Puttnam which was, if anything, more homo-erotic than anything between the leads in that limp-wristed travesty, *Gallipoli*. Even the perceptive Mr Ellis had missed the point.

Ashton's circus

During interval, while a few hundred rowdy midgets queue to buy ice creams from a dwarf in clown's make-up, the rouseabouts erect the cage for the lion tamer. The sections are lifted into place and braced, and a net is lowered from above and tied in place. This is to discourage the cats from climbing over the top and joining the audience. With a dressing gown over his costume, the young trainer, Tommy Chipperfield, walks around looking, shaking, testing. He carries a shovel which he uses to shift the sawdust, so that the steel sections can be bedded more firmly in the earth. Now he checks the folding seats for each of the cats, to make sure they're stable. The animals are nervous enough during performances without having wobbly seats. Finally it's time to position the big chromium stands on which they'll pose, from which they'll jump. And having done it all, he does it all over again. Apart from the danger to him, in the ring, no circus could afford to have these animals masticating the customers.

Founded in 1832, on the site of Sydney's Central Station, Ashton's has survived bushfires, floods, depressions, wars and, most dangerous of all, profound changes in public taste to celebrate this, its 150th year in Australia.

According to family history, they had to defend themselves against wild Aboriginals in the beginning, later making friends with some of the tribes.

In 1840 James Ashton trained an Aboriginal horseman, Mungo Mungo, to star in a bare-back act. A young Irishman called Ned Kelly sometimes watched the show, later enjoying a cuppa with the performers. Though the traditional March of the Gladiators is now contrasted with themes from TV shows, no military regiment is more conscious of its traditions.

The young man in the lion cage, who at last seems satisfied with the preparations, has family traditions too. Since the time of Charles II there have always been Chipperfields in British circuses. In 1649, Will Chipperfield worked the West Country street fairs, carrying a booth that folded into a sort of rucksack.

'The Ashtons are aerialists basically', Tom tells me in his caravan, 'whereas the Chipperfields have been animal trainers. Bears, monkeys, everything. The family would play in village squares. They even performed in the middle of the Thames when it was frozen over.'

Now the lions and tigers come running through the chute, roaring into the ring. One shows a little reluctance and Tom's girlfriend prods it with a stick. They take their places on their respective stools and sit glaring at Tom, now resplendent in his sequined suit.

There are two big male tigers, Zarak and Chandru, plus two young females, Kitty and Mowgli. The lionesses are Dahlia, Sita and Rosa and, compared to the tigers, look rather dowdy.

'I don't have male lions in the act', explains Tom, 'because they get too stupid when the females are on heat. Just don't know what they're doing. Male tigers have a different sexuality, so that's not a problem. What *is* a problem is that tigers are very different from lions and much harder to train. Lions are comparatively playful animals that are used to being together, so you can pile them up on each other and pull their manes or tails and they don't mind. But tigers are solitary animals. These ones don't even like each other.'

Zarak and Chandru take their turns leaping from stand to stand, Dahlia walks a plank and Sita jumps through a hoop. The act proceeds calmly and efficiently, in contrast to some of the others I've seen where the animals are forever clawing and snarling. Tom moves briskly around the ring, positioning his feet carefully, using his whip with economy of movement.

'There are cat trainers who drive the animals in front of them with the whip, whereas I prefer to bring the animals to me. It's a different approach altogether, and much more difficult ... You can bring a lioness towards you by touching it with a whip almost anywhere on the body. But you've got to be careful doing that to a tiger because it's just as likely to *keep* coming. I didn't train these animals myself. They've been trained to move fast, to keep running. Well, that's fine for lions but it's against the nature of tigers. You've got to let a tiger take its own pace if you want to get good results. So I'm trying to slow the act down, to pace it different. As a result they're fairly tense at the moment.'

'No, I've never been bitten.' He touches his head, for luck. 'I don't believe in that sort of thing. But there have been accidents in the family.' A Chipperfield was killed when performing in a cage and, more recently, they had to save a cousin from being mauled by leopards.

'It was a mixture of black and spotted leopards. He had a very dangerous part of the act where he'd lie on the ground and have a female leopard lie on top of him. Anyway, she was on heat and a male leopard got disturbed. All of a sudden he was buried in leopards. They were all over him, six of them. What you do is curl up, bring your knees to your chest and try to protect your face. He was lucky that we were all there. Soon the ring was full of Chipperfields and we got them off before he was too badly hurt. I miss having my family around me when I'm working here, in Australia. If anything did go wrong . . .'

A lioness jumps from stand to stand, instead of walking the plank. Tommy makes her do it again, but she jumps off halfway. 'I was going to make her do it a third time, but things were getting a bit edgy. The extraordinary thing about training animals is the way they'll do something over and over again for weeks, months or years. And then, suddenly, they'll *completely* forget. I suppose it's the same with people. It's strange, but it can happen in the middle of an act that you've done a thousand times. And when it does happen, you've got to start training them all over again, right from scratch.'

From scratch. Zarak takes a swipe at him on his way back to his stand. The paw is enormous and the growl sounds as if it's coming from some vast echo chamber, not simply an animal's throat. 'No, they're not that big. They're from Sumatra and there are far, far bigger tigers than that. The Russians, for example, train Siberian tigers and they're gigantic. I'd really like to specialise in tigers in the future because they're harder to train, to get to do real tricks. They're more of a challenge than lions.'

Advancing on a recalcitrant lioness with his whip handle, Tom persuades the temperamental lady to take her correct position in a tableau on the sawdust. She doesn't seem as amenable as all that. 'Still, it's the tigers you've got to watch. They're just not predictable.'

Nor, it seems, are pigs. Ashton's performing porkers were on in the first half. Lots of synchronised pink ones with a black-and-white spotted one providing comic relief. 'That's a very difficult act', says Tom. 'If you touch a pig with your whip and it squeals, the whole lot of them could turn on you. And did you see the camels? That's really very good. I've seen camel acts overseas where they didn't do much at all. But Gary really has those animals working well.' Lolloping around to the tune of 'In a Turkish Garden', high-humped and high-stepping, undulating swan-necks pushing forward supercilious faces, they looked for all the world like a dozen dowagers who've been dragooned into a chorus line.

According to the programme Tommy has trained bears, elephants, crocodiles, you name it. What animal has proved the most difficult? Horses, he says. 'They're so bloody stupid.' As well as the cats, Tommy does an act with a horse called Mephisto, with a girl pirouetting on its rump, evoking the sketches of Lautrec and Degas.

'The audience don't realise how difficult a horse act can be. At the moment it's even harder because I'm retraining the horse and the girl is new to the act. Actually, that's one of the disappointments about circus life — the really hard acts aren't always appreciated by the audience. For example, take a comic flyer, a clown up on a trapeze. That looks terribly easy but it's far, far harder than straight trapeze work. And my cousin who was mauled, he had a funny act with a black leopard who'd keep following him around the ring, refusing to go away. He'd push it away with his whip, and then turn his back and the thing would follow him like a pussy. Everybody laughed, but it was the most difficult part.'

Tommy was allowed into the family circus when he was sixteen, presenting acts that his father had trained. This included working with elephants which he regards as the easiest of animals. 'Mind you, teaching them to stand and pose, that's hard. You've actually got to *lift* them into position. You can't do it with a machine because there's no feel. So you've got to get underneath them and push them up with your arms until you feel they're balanced. Mind you, once they know the act, they simply go through the paces. *You* could get into the ring and do it. Of course, elephants are all different, just like any other animal. One will be fairly dull and simply go through the sequence. But another will really enjoy a performance and you can teach it new things.

'James Chipperfield bought a horse-drawn wagon in 1800, and that was the start of our proper circus. That's 180 years ago. In the 1960s we'd spend a year in Scotland, then a year in Wales, then a year in England. Or in Ireland. But nowadays there's so much competition. There are fifteen circuses touring England so you have to keep moving, go a hundred miles to do a show. And British audiences are tough. They just sit there staring at you. Australians like a circus a lot more. Just like the Africans.'

The Africans? Taking coals to Newcastle, Chipperfield toured Africa with lions, tigers and leopards. 'In other countries people don't think much of leopard acts because they're only little pussy cats. But in Africa, they know how dangerous leopards are. They are very enthusiastic.'

'In the wild, lions spend up to 20 hours a day asleep. They wake up for a while and do a bit of hunting, then they go straight back to sleep again. It's much the same in the circus. They sleep all the time and then wake up and do a performance, which is a substitute for hunting. Then they go straight back into the cage, have a yawn and they're asleep. It's ridiculous to talk about cruelty. Circus people aren't cruel to animals — although some circus people should know more about them. About their personalities and attitudes. Trainers who do understand what an animal's about get far better results.'

I compare it to sculpture, to the way a sculptor works within the nature of the material. Tommy agrees with the metaphor. 'That's *exactly* what you have to do, work with their temperament, not just push them around. You've got to really care for them.'

Tommy's commitment to his career, and to his animals, is confirmed by the books that are piled in every corner of the caravan — books on animals, novels about animals. 'What do you do for relaxation?' His girlfriend, who's busy making kewpie dolls for sale that afternoon, says 'He goes and does some extra training.'

'Well, you've got to', says Tommy, 'you should warm up a horse for an hour before you begin to train it, and then you've got to train it for an hour on its own. And you have to train every horse separately before you even put them in the ring together. When I go back to England, I want to have some new acts of my own. Some horses, but mainly tigers.'

And what if something *does* go wrong? What if something does happen? Pausing from sticking the kewpie dolls on wooden sticks, his girlfriend says: 'I'd just scream out "THEY'RE EATING TOMMY!" ', she laughs, not very convincingly. Because something could go wrong at any time, at any performance. Things *do* go wrong, despite all the careful preparation. Just a few weeks back Jonas, who does the dental act, dangling from the top of a tent while a girl spins from a mouth piece clenched in his jaws, had trouble with the rigging. Suddenly they both tumbled into the audience. The girl, Marilyn, comes into the caravan with her neck in a brace. 'We were lucky', she says, 'it was just at the beginning of the act. Otherwise . . .' And she pulls a face.

I've always loved the lingering fantasy of circuses, the variations on virtually unchanging acts. Bravely absurd and anachronistic, they continue to provide surrealism in the suburbs.

As Oscar Wilde wrote in 1889, when Ashton's had already been on the road (and off them, using Mungo Mungo as a tracker to find their way) for fifty years, 'A good circus is an oasis of Hellenism in a world that reads too much to be wise, and thinks too much to be beautiful.'

A final comment on Hitler's diaries

'It is by the promise of a sense of power that evil attracts the weak.'   Eric Hoffer, 1954

A final comment on Hitler's diaries. Despite all the disclaimers, they are completely genuine. Hitler was the forgery. The ghastly little führer was a figment of the German imagination. He gave the nation a scapegoat, someone to blame for their anti-semitism and self-destructive fantasies. Don't blame us, it was him. We Germans, like the Jews, gypsies and Jehovah's Witnesses, were his innocent victims.

I remember visiting Dachau, one of the first of the camps. By no means one of your major Nazi abattoirs. Not established for full-scale extermination, but hardly a Butlin's. (These days kids ride their bikes and play football inside the walls topped with rusting razor wire, and the local citizenry use the camp for short cuts on their way to go shopping.) And I was handed a little sheet of paper in which the municipality reminded one of its proud place in an earlier German history, of Dachau's cultural credentials. 'We knew nothing of what was going on here,' said the text. Odd that, given the way old, two-storey homes stand around the perimeter. It would be more plausible if the people of Jolimont claimed ignorance of what went on in the MCG.

But not to worry. Germany can blame the fictional Hitler for the holocaust just as mediaeval man could blame the fictional devil for sin. In that way you make evil something outside yourself, something alien. You can ignore the hypothesis of that Jewish swine Freud who suggested that a propensity for evil was inside us, as much a part of us as breathing.

Promoted by Goebbels, choreographed by Riefenstahl, this banal little man was totally fraudulent, a monstrous hoax. Shades of Oz when the fearsome Wizard is revealed as a sad, silly little man pulling levers. Hitler didn't use the German people for his purposes: they used him for theirs. He was a wish-fulfilment fantasy for people who wanted to see gods in their shaving mirrors. Consequently they forgot the humanity in the faces of their erstwhile friends and neighbours. Suffer the little children says the *New Testament*, so an ostensibly Christian nation suffered them all right — crushing them into cattle trucks and gas chambers in the Final Solution that John Bennett and revisionist historians tell us never happened. It is, of course, an Israeli fabrication for propaganda purposes.

Hitler was a figment of the German imagination as surely as Ronald Reagan was a figment of America's. (How could America possibly blame Reagan for anything? They knew he was a window dummy, a billionaire's marionette when they elected him.) Hitler was a hoax, a means by which the people could embrace unprecedented arrogance and hatred. Having burnt the books, they reduced ideas and philosophies to the status of talk balloons in comic strips, chanting 'Germans are the master race' and 'Jews eat Christian babies'. No, Hitler wasn't the reason for all this, but the excuse. We couldn't help it. We were powerless. We didn't know. We were only following orders.

(Incidentally, that's the problem of Bob Hawke's consensus. It seems that a society can't get its act together without having someone to hate. And Bob has taken away our enemies. Fraser had the unions, Menzies the communists, Holt those demonstrating students. Whitlam had Kerr. Now that Bob's brought Australia together there's no one to blame except ourselves.)

Borrowed from the Aryans of India, the swastika looks like a crucifix in jackboots. It stomped all over Europe grinding the innocent into the mud. Now it stomps through our unhealthy minds, exercising a terrible, sickening fascination. The bikies put swastikas on their jackets and helmets. The networks put swastikas on the screen and double the ratings. Authors put swastikas on their covers and become best-sellers. Whilst expressing outrage and horror, we're drawn to the mysteries of Nazism like protesting puritans leafing through porn. We're drawn to its menace like moths to the flame because, very simply, it's more *interesting* than virtue. More photogenic, more fun. So the neo-Nazis strut their stuff in Europe, the UK and America, cheering the memory of little Adolf, the superstar of sadism, the Elvis Presley of evil. The first media manipulated, mass-marketed leader, Hitler had no more authenticity than silly Ronnie Raygun. He was the Gerry Gee of Germany, not the führer of the Third Reich so much as the ventriloquial doll of an entire people.

Nazism remains big business because it appeals to the Nazi in all of us. Or in most of us. It represents the black hole of human emotion, the vortex into which all decency and rationality disappeared. Exploiting the pornography of violence (based on the inability of human beings to come to terms with mortality and death), Nazism festooned its uniforms with skulls and turned the world into a charnel-house. And that black hole still exists, still has the power to lure us. While porn cinemas and up-market films like *The Night Porter* use Nazism as an aphrodisiac, that's in recognition that the Second World War was the ultimate snuff movie. You see the iconography of Nazism creeping into punk rock and the promo clips on *Countdown*. Mind you, what do you expect when unemployment produces the same social tensions among the young that Nazism exploited and orchestrated?

Equally disturbing is the tendency to see nobility in Nazism. In that obscene apologia *Inside the Third Reich* by the smarmy Speer (and in a dozen pot-boiling books and movies like *Young Lions*) we're presented with the decent German officer who really hated Hitler — to the extent of heroically murmuring things behind his back like 'the rotten little Austrian upstart'. And we're programmed to see such men as splendid and courageous. After all, they have strong jaws and look really groovy in their uniforms.

There's even a tendency to keep reinterpreting Hitler as though the part was interchangeable with Hamlet. Derek Jacobi's sensitive, sentimental führer in the Speer series is a recent manifestation. God, we've had uncles who were more malevolent than that benevolent man in the bunker. Such a soft and romantic portrait. I half expected the Speer-and-Jacobi Hitler to burst into song like Jeanette MacDonald and Nelson Eddy.

Let us *never* forget what squalid, sordid little men these Nazis were. Once you pulled off their big, black boots they were midgets. Without Goebbels and Riefenstahl to amplify their egos, they were insects. Cambridge historian Norman Stone reminds us that 'he himself was a nervous wreck, stooped shouldered, all a-tremble. He quietened his nerves as best he could. In the Reich Chancellery were kept wooden models of the great Linz that was to be built. Hitler would sometimes stumble across the rubble in the gardens to go and inspect these models, with much gushing appreciation of the architect's design . . . His appetite for cake, always considerable, became quite ferocious . . . Discipline in the bunker began to slacken . . . People no longer rose when Hitler entered the room, nor did they automatically stop talking . . . Front officers with high decorations, who came to receive an honorific conversation with their leader and who would hope to put in an oar or two for sanity, would listen dumbfounded to his monologues . . . The strain was too much for Himmler, who knew nothing at all about war. He retired to a sanatorium at Hohenlychen, living on a diet of strychnine, belladonna and hormone tonic . . . He wanted to know from a Swede as "one man of the world to another, should I offer my hand to General Eisenhower when I meet him?" . . . There was a similar, extraordinary meeting between Himmler and the representative of the world Jewish organisation. Himmler suggested "It is time that we Germans and you Jews buried the hatchet".'

Our continuing interest in those mediocre men is grotesque. Confused by the theatricality of the Reich, we take them almost as seriously as they took themselves. Watching *Inside the Third Reich*, and reading the nonsense around the so-called diaries, I start to believe that Mel Brooks and Zero Mostel had the best idea in *The Producers*. While it might seem difficult or even blasphemous, the way to deal with the memory of Hitler and his pornographic political pantomime is to laugh at it.

The best things to inherit are good genes

As Bob Hawke once observed, the best things to inherit are good genes. Splendid chromosomes, dynamic DNA. Fortunately, the Adams family seethes with superior cells, as can be seen in the great successes my relatives have notched up in various fields. Great Uncle George founded Tattersalls in Tasmania, a form of voluntary taxation that now props up Victoria's Treasury. Second cousin Herbert, known to his friends as 'Sponge Fingers' and inspired by the family motto: 'Let them eat cake', went on to establish countless high-caloried emporia. Long before World Series Cricket's 'Come on Aussie, Come on', Melbourne's favourite rallying cry was 'The big men fly for a Herbert Adams pie'.

I was talking to Michael Parkinson about his own dynamic dynasty. Three brothers, each making a significant contribution to civilisation. From Fred, Bert and Mike came, respectively, Parkinson's law, Parkinson's disease and Parkinson's TV show.

Look at the Nolan family. One brother takes up the cudgels on behalf of the down-trodden worker, while the other takes up paint brushes on behalf of the social elite. And look at the Hamer boys. One becomes Premier of Victoria, another a much-admired Senator and the third goes to America to become a famous detective. You must have read of the adventures of Mike Hamer in the novels of Mickey Spillane.

And Mike isn't the only talented Australian to make it big in the US of A. Take the brilliant Boyds. Whilst many of them could be described as Boyds of a feather, one struck out in a quite unexpected direction. We have Arthur and David doing their daubs, Hermia and Guy tossing their pots while Robin tossed off the odd building and defined the Australian Ugliness. But we tend to forget about Bill Boyd who left Melbourne for Hollywood where he became famous as Hopalong Cassidy. For some reason the Boyds don't talk of Bill much although, frankly, I think they should be awfully proud. As a child I always found Hopalong a great inspiration. Sitting on his white horse wearing his big white hat, he symbolised everything good and decent. In much the same way that Ronnie Raygun, sitting in his White House, does today. In fact, if I had a hat, preferably a big white one, I'd take it off to Bill.

Incidentally, it's not generally known that when Bill sailed for Hollywood on P&O he was accompanied by another actor brother of an artist family. Yes, Rupert Bunny's brother, Bugs. Bugs, who died just a few years ago, became a star in his own right, making many shorter films for Warner Bros.

Bill Boyd, Bugs Bunny. Come to think of it, it's amazing how many children from famous Australian families made it big in Hollywood. Take Gene and Grace who fled the country after the police arrested their father, Ned. Taking their share of the loot, they set themselves up at Metro Goldwyn Mayer where they enjoyed spectacular careers. Gene is, I understand, now in semi-retirement, while Grace went on to become Queen of Tonga or some such place.

If we look at the Hughes we see Billy, the Prime Minister, and his talented actress daughter, Wendy. If we look at the Millers, there's Keith the cricketer, Max the comedian and Harry the entrepreneur. And we mustn't forget Harry's older brother Arthur who wrote a few obscure plays for Broadway. Not in the same street as *Hair* or *Jesus Christ Superstar*, they're modest little low-budget affairs like *Death of a Salesman* and *The Crucible*. However, Arthur achieved brief notoriety for marrying President James Monroe's daughter, Marilyn.

And it hasn't all been a one-way traffic. While we've lost a few talented sons to America, we've gained the odd immigrant. Take the famous Kennedy dynasty. After Jack and Bobby were assassinated, Rose Kennedy sent her two remaining sons to the Antipodes for safety. One became a popular TV compere and thespian while the other, Buzz, let everyone down by finishing up as one of those squalid newspaper columnists.

And no inventory of famous siblings should ignore Ranald and Ronald, the twin sons of Nelson Eddy and Jeanette

MacDonald who were also sent to Australia for safety during the Second World War. Ranald went on to become Managing Director of David Syme while Ronald has been a huge success in hamburgers.

Did you know that Don Lane was related to the Federal Minister, Tony Street? (I forget exactly where the families intersect.) That Bishop Fulton Sheen's younger brother went into the aerosol business? That Peter Weir's father was the famous engineer, Hume Weir? That Joan Crawford was Hector's first wife?

And what about that wonderful family, the Newtons. After a glancing blow from a Granny Smith, Uncle Isaac discovered gravity. Although fruit ran in the family (we mustn't forget Fig Newton), most of the Newtons have made their mark in show business. There's Wayne Newton, the Mafia's favourite singer who owns half of Las Vegas. There's Bert and his daughter Patti who make such a wonderful contribution to the Nine Network. And, of course, there's Olivia Newton-, the well-known chanteuse.

Mind you, there are a few sad stories. Andrew Peacock's brother only made captain in the British Army and, when last seen, had a menial job in *Are You Being Served?*

Given the Cook family's association with travel (Thomas Cook, Cook's Travellers Cheques and Cook's Tours) we can hardly be surprised that it was young James who went to see the Queen of Spain, borrowed *HMS Beagle* and discovered Australia.

And what of the Boyer family who gave us the lectures and Charles? And the Fords, who gave us the car and the pills? And Gertrude Lawrence's talented sons, D.H. and T.E., who gave us the dirty books and the desert? And the Howard brothers, Trevor, Leslie and John? While the older brothers appeared in big budget films, John appeared in big budget budgets.

It's absolutely amazing the way the same sort of talent — for painting pictures, making money — will run in a family. For instance, look at the way royalty runs in the Windsors. For a time there the Windsors were so extraordinarily royal that they had to open branch offices in Russia and Germany. Frankly, I find it astonishing the way that everyone in the family, even the smallest children, are royal. It's remarkable the way regal qualities are encoded in the genes. Princes, Princesses, Dukes, Duchesses, I doubt that there's a commoner amongst the lot of them. And not content with opening flower shows or unveiling plaques, the Royal family has spread around the world making their mark in so many fields. Look at Hal Prince, one of the most successful producers on Broadway. And our own Bernard King of recipe fame.

Yes, the Windsors remind me of the Pope family who have been running the Vatican for generations. Pope succeeding Pope, down through the centuries. While one of the Popes went into the appliance business, the rest have stayed resolutely with religion which isn't surprising as, by and large, they're Catholics. How proud the original Mr and Mrs Pope would be if they could see how the Vatican has remained a family business.

STOP PRESS:
It has come to my attention that there's been a long history of dissension among Australia's leading cultural dynasty, the Lindsays. Daryl didn't approve of Norman, Lionel didn't approve of Daryl and now, it seems, Joan doesn't approve of Reg. Just because he sings hillbilly songs.

The Year of the Tree

In China, it is the Year of the Dog. In Australia, they tell me, it's the Year of the Tree. Tree, *n*. 1 A woody, perennial plant with one main stem or trunk which develops many branches. 2 A gallows. 3 The cross on which Jesus was crucified (archaic).

The Tree, which inspired one Joyce Kilmer to write: 'I think that I shall never see a poem as lovely as a'. (He continued in fine style, with 'poems are made by fools like me, but only God can make a tree'.)

But while Joyce was in fine voice, my favourite poetic reference to the tree comes from the famous Eccles in a vintage Goon Show. 'I talk to the trees,' he sang, 'that's why they put me away'. That being the case, they should also have jailed Bismarck who used to leave important Prussian meetings so that he could invigorate himself by embracing a trunk or three. By hugging a tree, Bismarck found himself revived, ready for more blood, sweat and tears. One hopes that hugging them is all he did, that he didn't seek out trees with knot holes and perform some vegetarian variant on bestiality.

Mind you, I'd quite understand it if he did, as, like Joyce, Eccles and Otto, I *love* trees. We bought the house we live in simply because it had a magnificent tree, a veritable explosion of chlorophyll, in the front garden. A Morton Bay with elephant-grey bark, it evoked memories of the sacred banyan trees of India and Bali. Soaring up and out, it took the house under one of its great, green wings. One of the saddest moments of my life was when I discovered, soon after moving in, that the tree would have to be cut down as, for all its lusciousness, its massive trunk had all but rotted through.

I think back to the trees of my childhood. As a kid, I lived with my grandparents, sleeping in a bungalow surrounded by pines and peppercorns. I used to find mushrooms amongst the dusty needles of the pines and spent days on end up the peppercorns, pretending to be Tarzan. One peppercorn used to feel like a giant hand and I'd sit in its palm surrounded by its great finger-branches. This gave me a view over the footpath where I could look down at people walking by, forever astonished at how odd humans look from above, at how long a step is. When my grandfather died the place was sold and they cut down the peppercorn. Marvellous as he was, I think I mourned the tree almost as much as the man.

At school, a row of gums stood at the edge of the asphalt playground. We spent hours there, on our knees, playing with our Dinky cars in the dust. Digging under the roots so we'd have bridges. And after school, in the summer, we'd run down to the Yarra and swing like Weissmullers from ropes tied to the branches of river gums. The bright blue, chlorinated backyard pools have destroyed that experience of childhood, of arcing out over mud-brown water which, just as often, you shared with a desperately swimming snake. And once or twice, a frightened platypus.

Sadly the part of the river that we most enjoyed, where we'd dive-bomb each other from the upper branches, has now been destroyed by one of those 'rivers of concrete', a stream of traffic, being the F19 Freeway.

I can remember walking with my cousin Terry along the now-buried riverbanks and seeing where Aboriginals had cut canoes from the living bark. And we left the signs of our culture beside the long-leaf-shaped cuts, by adding our initials. Sometimes we'd eat the witchetty grubs we found beneath the bark, evoking the mystery of a long-vanished people.

Later, living in Eltham, I had another favourite tree, a tall gum with torn, ragged bark where I'd hide from my loony stepfather. I remember the way the branches moved in the wind, making me feel that I was adrift in some endless ocean. Now the green horizons of surging, waving grass have been subdivided into building lots, though the tree survives, its branches hacked back so there's little more than a stump. Apparently the new owner didn't want leaves in his spouting.

On the way to Eltham High there was a fallen tree that formed a bridge over our creek. We imagined ourselves tight-rope walkers as we crossed it with tentative footsteps, running the last few yards to safety. And at the back of our school were the vestiges of an old quince orchard which became our Sherwood Forest, a place to hide from teachers and prefects. It was here that we'd pick rock-hard quinces for magnificent gladiatorial combats, the famous quanger fights. We'd pinch all the galvo lids off the dustbins and use them for shields — from fruit flung with such force that it would bruise flesh or dent the metal.

We'd make canoes from sheets of galvanised iron and paddle these wobbly craft through the trailing filaments of willow trees. No wonder they're called weeping willows — there's something about them that's almost absurdly poignant.

And, of course, there were tree huts. Rickety nests made from discarded crates, which we could occupy in secret elitism. Arboreal Melbourne Clubs, the perfect place to reveal our fantastical ambitions.

As I sit here at the typewriter, tapping out words on paper made from a tree, to be printed on paper made from a forest, I find my mind wandering back to that first peppercorn. I can still climb it in my memory, feeling familiar nooks and crannies for feet and knees. Thirty years later, its branches evoke the safety of parental arms. And I look down to see the iceman arriving, trimming a block with his ice pick and lugging it beneath me, balanced on a hessian sack on his shoulder, lugging it towards my grandma's kitchen door. And here comes the Jellis bakery cart, magnificently painted in scarlet and gold. From my vantage point I see my father arriving home on leave, climbing out of a cab in his army uniform. I use the tree as a refuge from the local bully and see the first Holden driving down High Street. God, it wasn't just a peppercorn — it was like a whole series of *The Sullivans*.

A few weeks ago I drove through the Dandenongs, looking at the great trees burned to death in the 1939 bushfires. And we drove through a valley where, generations back, they grew trees for the masts of schooners. Pushing up towards the light, the trunks were so tall and straight that they could carry a schooner around the world. Which reminds me of flying over the hills of Lebanon and looking down at the few surviving cedars left over from the forest plundered by the ancient Egyptians for their buildings and carvings. And I also remember walking through the Gothic cathedrals of Canada's redwoods, amongst trees that contain all recorded history, from the Pharaohs to the Presidents, in their concentric rings. Trees that refresh the air we breathe and that lay down their lives for our homes, our heat and our furniture.

In the corner of the room there's an African chieftain's throne from the Cameroons, carved from a single tree. It's a massive affair, as old as the hills, made up of human faces and the intertwined bodies of leopards. It must have taken centuries to grow and has had a second life, for centuries, as a work of art. Beside it are a couple of Egyptian carvings, 4,000 years old, where the wood is still so, well, woody that it might have been carved this morning. And above them painted on a twisting, buckling panel is a 17th century image of the Madonna and child, a painting on a piece of wood from a tree that grew, God knows where, in Tsarist Russia. Wood, so responsive to tools and the human imagination, from forests that no longer exist.

There are still a few trees in our garden that were planted 120 years ago. A couple of vast, dark pines that sough in the wind and two ancient magnolias that put out flowers the size of dinner plates. And hardly a week goes by when we don't plant more trees, hoping that they, too, will survive a century.

Such plantings make me think of, and respect, the Englishmen who planted oaks and elms in grand designs for gardens that they could never live to see. Gardens which survived until the last few decades, only to be devastated by the Dutch Elm disease.

We're cutting down the bush in Australia, devastating the last rain forests and flooding the valleys. There's something peculiarly Australian about the sight of a man-made lake full of drowned trees, holding up their branches in the air like swimmers calling for help that never comes. And the same dams that hold back the water prevent the annual flooding that nurtured our red gums so that they will soon join the growing list of endangered species, the rare woods that are being replaced by the ubiquitous and suffocating conifers. I'm not one of those who hate foreign trees, who believe in terrorist ring-barking attacks, who argue for a White Australian Tree Policy. But it is saddening to see our landscape being converted into a pale imitation of Europe's. No two gum trees are the same, but if you've seen one conifer, you've seen them all.

In a way, the wheel has come full circle. On the wall of my study there's an old leather screen showing Captain Cook arriving in Australia where he's met by a lot of spear-waving Hottentots who bear not the slightest resemblance to Aboriginals. And the landscape behind them is dominated by trees from a European experience, the unmistakable shape of oaks. It took centuries before the painters of this continent could forgive Australia for its gums or its light. Until artists could finally see beauty in the unfamiliar, our bush was so distorted by prejudice that it finished up looking like Hyde Park.

Now, after the era in which we discovered the beauty of the indigenous trees, the mass-produced pines seem to be taking over. I fear for the future. Perhaps the time will come when

Australians will have to travel to California or to Israel to see a decent stand of eucalypts.

Since I planted the trees many varieties of birds that we haven't seen since childhood have returned, even cockatoos and parrots. And I resolve to keep planting trees anywhere and everywhere I can. For birds to nest in, for kids to climb, for air to breathe.

There's a New England proverb that says 'The forest is the poor man's overcoat'. And an old English proverb that says 'He that plants trees loves others beside himself'. And in a world where our population increases as fast as the forests recede, a useful motto for the next few centuries might be 'Less people, more trees'.

FOOTNOTE:
A few years back, the Allegheny County Commissioners decided to cut down two thirds of the trees surrounding the Joyce Kilmer Memorial at South Park because 'the trees obscured the memorial and prevented visitors from reading his famous lines'.

Dramatic compofition fet to mufic

'No good opera plot can be sensible, for people do not sing when they are feeling sensible.' W.H. Auden, 1961

'Opera, noun. A play representing life in another world, whose inhabitants have no speech but song, no motions but gestures and no postures but attitudes.'
Ambrose Bierce, *The Devil's Dictionary*, 1900

'Nothing is capable of being well set to music that is not nonsense.' Joseph Addison, 1710

Braving the savage silver fish that lurk within, I open my trusty, dusty Britannica seeking a definition of opera. And I find that it's a 'dramatic compofition fet to mufic, and fung on the stage, accompanied with mufical inftruments, and enriched with magnificent dreffes, machines, and other decorations'. Frankly, I suspect our edition of the Britannica isn't entirely up to date — not when it defines medicine as 'the art of preferving health when prefent, and of restoring when loft'. Similarly with Panama, 'the capital city of the province of Darian in Fouth America, where its treafures of gold and filver, and other rich merchandise of Peru, are lodged in magazines till they are fent to Europe'. The salesman that came to our door must have been selling old stock.

Further delving revealed that opera's birth date is fixed in the year 1600, when Jacapo Peri's *Euridice* was performed in Florence, though in the Middle Ages, and even earlier 'there existed combinations of music and dramatic action which may be regarded as its forerunners'. And during the Renaissance, plays were written with a chanting or reciting chorus on the model of ancient Greek drama. (I'm puzzled by the failure of reference books to list *Aida*, the *Oklahoma!* of ancient Egypt. I understand that it ran for a record-breaking three dynasties at the Karnak theatre in Thebes.)

All this scholarly stuff is to introduce the fact that, this year, I've been attending the Australian Opera's productions in Melbourne and having a *ripper* time. (The trick is not to read the critics next morning who insist that you had a rotten time.) Until my wife bullied me into buying some season tickets, I'd always regarded opera as both over-priced and over-subsidised, a form of cultural ostentation enjoyed by an insufferably pompous elite. I now realise that I've been guilty of the most shameful philistinism, and that opera combines the energy of a League premiership with the razzle-dazzle of *Sale of the Century* and the unbridled emotionalism of Greeks farewelling a flight at Tullamarine.

Bruce Beresford used to drag me off to operas in London — stark, modern stuff by Benjamin Britten and his ilk. This had me asleep within seconds but, to be perfectly fair, *all* forms of theatre produce irresistible drowsiness. I was the *Bulletin*'s theatre critic for many years and slept through more productions at St Martin's and the MTC than I care to remember.

(Not that this stopped me writing the most savage and devastating reviews.) I've also slept through productions of *Evita* in New York and London, and Maggie Smith's famous impersonation of Virginia Woolf at the Hippodrome. It's true I did zzz off a few times at Melbourne's Princess, as dirigible-sized divas got overwrought, adding their physical flambuoyancy to the flamboyant goings-on. But for most of the season my attention was riveted.

For example, in this era of agonising amplification, when the miniscule talents of musicians tend to be magnified through microphones, it is remarkable to hear the nude voice, as it were, filling the entire Princess Theatre. A little trembling doover in the throat producing enough soundwaves to loosen fillings from the front stalls to the back row of the gods. Then there's the surprising pulchritude of the performers. Whilst some of the stars are traditionally amplitudinous, to the extent that they make yours truly look like Twiggy, there's a generation of tenors and sopranos who can only be described as spunks. (That's a word frequently used by my teenage daughters and seems to have superseded 'heart throb'.) On a number of occasions I watched my wife sitting forward in her seat, entranced by the charms of some Prima Don, Dick or Harry. The mere mention of Anson Austin, a young New Zealand tenor, and a faraway look appears in her eyes, accompanied by a mysterious, Giaconda smile. And I am similarly affected and afflicted by memories of Anne-Maree McDonald.

The argument that opera seats are expensive is absurd. I mean, it costs you a couple of hundred dollars to fly to Sydney in an aluminium cylinder, accompanied by a pilot, a first officer and three hosties. Whereas for 25 bucks the Australian Opera will fly you to Florence, Venice or 19th century Kyoto with a conductor, full orchestra, 300 singers and four changes of set. Frankly, I don't know how they do it for the money.

Admittedly they've been getting subsidies from the Australia Council and private corporations. For example, the *Sydney Morning Herald* sponsored *Otello* and in the opening scene the famed Aboriginal was looking up shipping movements in the

Classifieds. Katies subsidised *Manon Lescaut*, requiring only a brief burst of their 'K-k-k-Katies' jingle in the second act. The Jim Beam Opera Foundation underwrote *Falstaff* on the condition that the well-upholstered star quaffed Bourbon instead of mead, while the smoke that wafted across the set in *War and Peace* was provided by the Benson and Hedges Company. Olivetti underwrote *La Boheme* and their involvement was admirably low-key — just the sound of a Lettera 22 clicking away as the tenor typed out 'Your tiny hand is frozen'.

At the beginning of this article, I quoted a few cynical observations by opera-haters of the past. For my own part, I'll side with Lord Chesterfield who said 'Whenever I go to an opera, I leave my sense and reason at the door with my half guinea, and deliver myself up to my eyes and my ears'. For far from being absurd and artificial, I find opera totally accurate and realistic. For in my experience, the most emotional moments of one's life, involving grief, love, jealousy, rage and what have you, are wholeheartedly operatic. There *is* a full orchestra hammering away in your lounge room, bedroom or whatever. The big emotions are hair-tearing, bosom-wrenching and tympani bashing. Which is why the cinema has borrowed so heavily from opera, almost burying the images in lush orchestrations. Your abstract, intellectual arguments are comparatively bloodless affairs and take place to the accompaniment of yawns. But the surging, extravagant emotionalism of human affairs *demands* the wholehearted support of a Puccini or Verdi. Indeed, almost every week my wife and I have an argument on the scale of the 1812 Overture, before making up to *Swan Lake*.

Which brings me to this year's production of that extraordinary piece of work, which wrung more emotions out of me than I thought I had. Surely I was too cynical, too world-wise, blasé and supercilious to be touched by that old pot-boiler. Not so. I had to be led out of the Princess by two ushers, applying nose to sleeve as I blubbered helplessly. Weeks later I can't look a bonsai tree or zen flower arrangement in the eye without dissolving into tears.

The trouble with Bill

After Gough was crucified by Pontius Kerr and ascended bodily into heaven, the Labor Caucus decided that they didn't really want a leader again, as they tended to get a bit obstreperous. (Make no mistake about it, when Gough was good he was very, very good but when he was bad he made Josef Stalin look like Dale Carnegie.) So they elected a somewhat reluctant Bill Hayden to be first among equals, one of the boys, a man of consensus rather than command. Bob Hawke? Out of the question. Apart from the fact that he had yet to serve a parliamentary apprenticeship, he might 'do a Whitlam' and start throwing his weight around. In contrast, Hayden didn't have a lot of weight, but was trustworthy, decent and likeable.

And for a time, polls notwithstanding, Caucus was happy with their choice. While the Hawke circled above, ready to dive, Labor MPs convinced each other that they'd made the right decision. I was told how well Caucus committees were going, how people who'd felt bullied or intimidated by Whitlam were now emerging, contributing.

Yet I kept remembering a speech I'd given to the Fabian Society during the Calwell era, explaining why a leader like Arthur couldn't win a modern election. To a chorus of hisses and boos, I'd insisted that we didn't have Federal elections any more, but pseudo-Presidential elections, where people voted for a leader rather than a local candidate. Indeed, in most cases they had no idea who the local candidate was, converting a vote for Bob or Arthur into local terms with their how-to-vote cards.

So as to dramatise the choice confronting my fellow Fabians, I told the story of the Democrat candidate who approached Tammany Hall for campaign funding in the 1930s. He was confronted by a little guy chewing on a cigar who, coolly assessing the candidate, asked him a question. 'Have you ever seen the Staten Island ferry coming in? Seen the way it sucks in all the rubbish and the dead cats and the Coca Cola bottles in its wake?' The candidate had acknowledged that he had. 'Well, Franklin Delano Roosevelt is your Staten Island ferry. We'll spend the money on *his* campaign.'

I pointed out that Menzies, more like the *Queen Mary* than a mere ferry, was running presidential elections, completely overshadowing the other candidates, including his own Ministers, and forcing the voters into harsh appraisals of the Calwell alternative. I insisted that the impact of television would require leaders who were *performers*, who were at home on the box. And I recall unveiling the Theory of Political Natural Selection, which tended to produce world leaders of fairly impressive appearance, frequently larger than life. De Gaulle, Mao Tse Tung, Soekarno, Stalin, Kennedy, Nasser — all had 'charisma', a terrible word that was not, as yet, in vogue.

Even those who were smaller-than-life, be they Napoleon, Hitler, Krushchev or Bolte, were not exactly lacking in self-assurance. In such a world, Arthur Calwell had Buckley's hope of being a Prime Minister. Particularly when the working-class was producing a high incidence of Alf Garnetts ready to tug the forelock at Sir Robert. I played the Fabian conference some interviews I'd taped in factories where working men complained about Calwell's dress sense ('you can't wear yellow socks with a blue suit') and worried about him lunching with the Queen ('he wouldn't know which knife and fork to use').

Well, twenty years later, the same applies to Bill Hayden. And I'm not referring to yellow socks or bad table manners. It's just that I can't see the Australian voters electing him PM. Even if the Caucus was for him 100 per cent, the public have made their judgment. Old Testament propaganda notwithstanding, too few Davids topple Goliaths.

The trouble with Bill is that he's the bloke next door, and who wants to vote for the bloke next door? He might make quite a good PM in the way that Harry M. Truman made a surprisingly good President. But in the era of electronic electioneering, a Harry M. Truman is a charming anachronism. He wouldn't get elected. He wouldn't even get the nomination.

In any case, the Caucus isn't 100 per cent behind Bill. Indeed, the pollies who were most enthusiastic about him a few years back are now shaking their heads in sorrow. 'He's so bloody negative', says one. 'God help us with a Hayden budget', says another, 'he seems to think the money's *his*. You'd never get him to spend a quid on anything'. There's a feeling of listlessness, of depression. 'We were sitting around the other day at a Shadow Cabinet meeting', I was told, 'looking at each other in growing misery. God, what would happen if we actually won?'

In 1972 Gough Whitlam was much, much more than the Staten Island ferry. He was at very least the *QE2*. A few years later, sad to say, he became the ALP's *Titanic*. And on that navigational scale, Bill Hayden is, let's face it, an oarless dinghy.

The one bloke who could give Fraser a run for his money (or rather, *our* money) is Robert J. Hawke. Well, why is the Labor Party so reluctant to elect the most popular politician of the decade? It's not simply because they're still licking their wounds from the Whitlam years — aspects of Bob's character seem to frighten them. Almost everyone acknowledges his ability to win a forthcoming election, but they're worried about the sort of PM he might become.

It isn't the grog — he's got that under control and the public respected his candour. It's not his outbursts of aggression — these are less frequent. Nor is it his occasional emotionalism over issues like Israel. All of these facets have simply added to the public interest in a man of unusual complexity. There is some concern about his proclivity for harakiri — whether he's on self-destruct at a Party conference or telling the Madam Gandhi joke to an audience of feminists and diplomats. Oddly the public embrace and accept all this, and more, in Hawke. They know he's a rare talent for being his own worst enemy but they recognise his instinctive understanding of how they, as Australians, feel about issues and about themselves. And no one could call Hawke plastic, the product of manipulative image-making.

But within the ALP there's a resistance to Hawke that must be allayed if he's to beat a Keating, or even a compromise candidate like Bowen, in a spill. It's the fear of Bob and his Powerful Friends. To explain this anxiety, it would be helpful to consider the views of the English radical, Tony Benn, who says there are only three types of political leaders (a) straight men, (b) fixers, and (c) maddies. In the English context, Jim Callaghan's a straight man, Harold Wilson's a fixer and Margaret Thatcher is mad. The Australian context is full of straight men — Cain, Thompson, Howard, with Wran as the archetypal fixer and Bjelke-Petersen and Fraser as maddies. (I should point out that Benn and I are using 'maddies' in the sense of ideologues who actually want to drag society in one direction or pull it in another.) Applying the Benn test, Hawke is clearly a fixer, someone who would seek to use his network of influential mates to sort out social problems. It is, after all, a technique he used for years in ACTU negotiations, ringing up Sir this or Sir that to sort things out.

Well, there are many people in the ALP who mistrust a man who's so at home in the Members' stand at Flemington, who's on first name terms with the *Who's Who* of capitalism. On the other hand, it's this ability to move freely between the social classes that gives Hawke much of his popularity with the ordinary voter. (Our Alf Garnetts think it's beaut.) But what the public sees as pragmatism, as an ability to talk straight and free himself from ideological thinkers, can be viewed with suspicion in the party machine and in Caucus.

But mightn't this ability to reach consensus be just the talent we need in the rocky, difficult years that lie ahead? In the choice between fools, fanatics and fumblers, give me a fixer every time.

Even among Victoria's right-wing MPs and Senators, who *should* be Hawke enthusiasts, there's a tendency to doubt his real abilities. They see Bob's reputation as being exaggerated, a result of theatrical stunts. 'Bob had an ability to come into a crisis just before it was about to resolve itself', one told me, 'which gave him the reputation of being magical in negotiations. But he'd pick his issue and he'd pick his time . . . Well, a Prime Minister can't be that choosy. There are too many issues, too many crises. A PM is like one of those Chinese jugglers with bowls on sticks of bamboo. He's rushing up and down the stage twirling all the time, so that none of them gets the wobbles and falls off.'

Be that as it may, I've often seen Hawke walk into a room full of people and within seconds take command. Like it or not, he's a natural leader in a country crying out for leadership.

Which brings us to his performance as a Parliamentarian. Although MPs agree that Parliament is going down the tubes, that it's less and less important, they'd still like a leader who can keep the plates twirling in pure, parliamentary terms. And I'm forever being told of how Bob buggered up this or that by a lack of familiarity with parliamentary forms and protocol.

Perhaps that's right, but Bob will learn the tricks of the Parliamentary trade whereas Bill Hayden, sadly, cannot learn to capture the public imagination and command the attention of the media. The impact of media on Australian politics has been to create, for good or ill, a focus of attention on the leader — and Hayden is as strickened in that spotlight as one of the kangaroos in *Wake in Fright*.

Add it all up, and the aggregate of criticisms of Bob Hawke loom like Ayers Rock. But the fact remains that so does Bob Hawke. He towers over the political landscape and has survived every attempt to count him out. All those criticisms of Hawke have their elements of truth — yet none of them disqualifies him from his claim for leadership. If you were to write a list of Malcolm Fraser's shortcomings, you'd need a few sheets of foolscap. Arrogance, dogmatism, ruthlessness, etc., etc., etc. Yet there's no denying he's been one of the more formidable figures in our political history.

I've no doubt that Hawke's leadership would be turbulent and often traumatic. Oddly enough, the electorate knows that already. It knows what a complex, difficult bastard the man can be and yet it chooses to admire him. They see in Hawke some of the larrikin qualities they enjoyed in Gorton and they're aware that there's something just a little dangerous about the man. But they find him interesting and challenging in contrast to the dullness and decency of a Hayden.

In any case, if Hawke doesn't get the leadership, how will the ALP explain that to its party membership? More importantly, how will the party explain it to the voters at large? If Hawke doesn't lead the party, and lead it soon, a lot of Labor support will just fade, fade, fade away. It seems that the ornithological conflict between a Hawke and a Peacock may never take place, but in Hawke Malcolm Fraser will confront someone in his own weight division. Put Hayden against Fraser and you'd have the sort of unequal combat we haven't seen since McMahon tackled Whitlam.

The Victorian ALP will back Hawke reluctantly in the leadership tussle, if only because they prefer him to a Keating. Frankly, they have no other choice. And as far as I can see, looking around the field of candidates, nor has Australia.

Kew, Cemetery of the Month

What I spent, I had;
What I gave, I have;
What I kept, I lost.

An old Cornish epitaph

They're removing grandma's grave to build a sewer
They're removing it regardless of expense
They're removing her remains
To lay down sewage drains
To satisfy the local residents.

Peter Sellers's song

While everyone else is involved in the rowdy worship of the inflated bladder, I go to a Grand Final of a different kind, wandering lonely as a cloud amongst the headstones at Kew, my Cemetery of the Month.

Like chess pieces sliding off a rumpled table cloth, Kew's angels and obelisks teeter down the hill, only their wing tips and ben-ben (the term shall be explained later) visible over the high brick fence. A fence which invariably poses the same question: Is it to keep the living out or the dead in? One suspects the latter, given that the bucking tombs and heaving paths suggest much seething, subterranean activity. It's as though the RIPs (the VIPs of death) are struggling out of their coffins, rearing to go at the last trump. If so, we should forgive them their impatience. It's the boredom that does it. The Second Coming is such a long time coming.

I pick up an alphabet of wafer-thin lead letters that have fallen from an old inscription. L, B, E, C, R, K, T, E, A, R, R. Sorrowful Scrabble pieces, they once spelt ERBERT CLARK (his 'H' still clings to the headstone). Alongside, looking like a giant set of teeth, there's a row of identical stones gone mossy from want of brushing. The fang in the middle has broken off and fallen backwards. Though Kew is amongst the best kept of neighbourhood necropoli, many of the larger monuments have

been undermined and more than one giant crucifix needs to be urgently crucified. Given the disintegration of these modern products of monumental masonry, one can but marvel anew at the durability of the ruins of Greece and Rome.

Quite apart from the bronze greyhound lying on a bronze

cushion, forever keeping watch over a dead child, there are two extraordinary tombs here at Kew, one proud and the other poignant. The former is the last resting place of the *Age*'s David Syme, and some of his dynasty, occupying a choice piece of this unreal estate — right at the top of the hill near the main gates and clock tower. Hewn from massive granite blocks, it mocks at Methodism, pooh-poohs Presbyterians and shows a withering contempt for the Catholics. For it eschews Christian iconography in favour of, of all things, the Egyptian.

Yes, here in the middle of a decent, god-fearing Melbourne suburb is a Pharaonic temple, its lotus-columns crawling with bronze scarabs, Egypt's sacred beetles. (The slow-moving insect is one of the disguises of the arcing Sun, forever dying and forever being reborn.) And above there's a frieze of cobras, the Pharaonic emblem. As the African cobra can spit its venom two metres at a victim's eyes, one wonders at Syme's venomous intent. His temple must have outraged decent opinion both for its arrogance and its paganism.

Mind you, quite unwittingly Christians have filled their cemeteries with far more heretical symbols, the exclamation marks of the obelisk, topped by their little pyramids.

The Egyptian Genesis has the self-created Ra-Atum emerging from the Primordial Waters of chaos. With no place to stand, he creates a hillock to support him. This Primaeval Hill, this first mount of dry land, is in the shape of the pyramid — otherwise known as the ben-ben. Standing upon it, Ra-Atum creates his first pair of gods, Shu ('air') and Tefnut ('moisture') from his own semen. Masturbatory monoliths! How very unseemly in a Christian context.

Syme's cobras find their echo in the second tomb. At each corner of what must be the most remarkable grave in Australia (if you discount Walter Lindrum's monument at Melbourne General, a bronze billiard table complete with metal balls, cues and pockets), they are used as gargoyles, hissing their hatred of gossip and innuendo. For according to myth, this most romantic of buildings was borne out of the malice of neighbours.

Apparently a young doctor had married a very rich lady and,

upon her death, came into a spectacular inheritance. 'He married her for her money', mouths murmured behind lace-gloved hands, turning his grief into rage. And so he spent every last penny on building this most lavish of last resting-places.

Above its glinting black columns is a dome of rose-coloured glass, broken here and there by vandals' stones. Beneath it, the angel of death, standing on tip-toe, bends over his beloved whose halo, sadly, has been souvenired. On each side of the bier, in inlaid brass and art nouveau style, are the impassioned outpourings of the husband, the most ardent professions of love.

I cannot find a name anywhere. But I read that:

'TWELVE YEARS OF EARTH'S BEST LOVED
LIE BURIED HERE.
BORN ON THE 26th DAY OF JANUARY 1867
MARRIED ON THE 26th DAY OF JANUARY 1887
BURIED ON THE 26th DAY OF JANUARY 1897.'

The place is at once preposterous and painful and we are told it left him destitute. Let us hope that this sonnet in stone deeply shamed his critics.

There's more to fashion than hairstyles and hems. Even tombs can be trendy. For me, the Melbourne Cemetery has been ruined by the vulgarity of our Greeks and Italians. Forgetting the inspiration of Forum and Acropolis, their graves look like a cross between LTD hearses and fish-shop windows. Dead faces on ceramic tiles. Plastic flowers. Even little electric lights. And at Melbourne General, long since chocka, they've got them double-parked on the driveways.

And there's fashion in names. Both Christian and Sur. Kew has scores that have fallen out of use and, walking along, I find myself speaking them out loud.

Grace, Charlotte, Ada, Elsie, Selwyn, Hanna, Myrtle, Nellie, Maud, Gertrude, Florrie, Emma, Ernest, Hanibal, Ivy, Matilda, Jessie, Blanche, Minnie, Fanny, Arabella, Violet, Madge, Cornelius, Cora, Ambrose, Ebenezer, Agnes, Hettie.

Names like that aren't causing many ripples in the christening fonts these days.

Yes, most of them are women's as men tended to have sturdier, simpler designations, worn like sensible suits. John William, James, Thomas.

THIS TABLET WAS ERECTED BY THE SERVANTS AND DEPENDANTS OF A KIND AND INDULGENT CHRISTIAN LADY IN 1869.

And wrecked by vandals in 1969.

Row upon row of single beds, but here and there there's a double bed designed for married couples. Frequently only one of the partners is in residence. What happened to hubby or wife? Did they go away and die somewhere else? Did they remarry? Or did they choose cremation, having restless memories of the hubby's snoring?

In contrast, less affluent couples have been buried one on top of the other, bunk-style.

Here and there are mass graves for the monasteries and convents. The longevity of the fathers is an excellent advertisement for their reflective lives. All those marvellous innings! 79, 84, 92. Only one young chap let the team down, ruining the high-scoring average by being clean-bowled at 32.

The nuns lie under their adopted names. Sister Mary of the Sacred Heart McKillop, Sister Mary of the Purification Sheridan, Sister Mary of the Heart of Mary Kerin.

And here's a grave for Patrick White! Now, there's an interesting idea. Recycling old tombs for namesakes. Or alternately, having mass-graves to accommodate all the Patrick Whites, Max Harrises and David McNicolls. Wandering around I find a dozen old headstones that, dates aside, would be ideal for friends or contemporaries. And a couple of them are splendid — a shrouded urn on a tall pedestal and, rising even higher, a finger pointing optimistically at heaven.

At Kew, the splendour of the tombs is proof of affluence, of upward mobility that survives the death bed. Yet, regretfully, there's a poverty of epitaphs. That great joy of the English churchyard cannot be found.

For all that, the most compelling headstone I've seen was the simplest. My wife found it twenty years ago while we were wandering in the Oakleigh Cemetery, now defunct. The plainest piece of stone, devoid of decoration, with just these words.

THIS IS ELLEN'S GRAVE

No dates, no surname. And when we heard that the Oakleigh Council was (shades of Sellers's song) levelling the place for a car park, burying the cemetery beneath a shroud of asphalt, we hurried back to where a few broken headstones had been leaned against a fence, determined to take Ellen's home with us. But it wasn't there. It had been crushed by the bulldozer.

My last image of Kew Cemetery is that of Saskia, my six-year-old daughter. She's borrowed an empty jar from a neighbouring grave and half-filled it with water from a leaking tap. Now she arranges a handful of onion flowers in the jar and places it on the grave of her great-great-grandmother. The sight of this little girl, wholly absorbed in her flower arranging, makes me call her name. Looking up, she forgets to be sad and runs laughing towards me, skipping along the broken upheaval of the path. As I feel a similar upheaval in my mind and my heart.

A feeling of history

You can get a feeling of history from postage stamps, old newspaper headlines, snatches of pop songs, the changing styles of painting, feature films or architecture. You can see history in the evolution of the motor car — as the chromium fangs and dorsal fins of the 1950s shrink into the four-wheeled shopping trolley of today. You can see history in the way trousers flare, tighten or flop — in the way hair rises like yeast (to be pressure-pak lacquered) or falls as loose as morals.

But I prefer the record left by words like these . . .

'The order is rapidly fadin'
And the first one now will later be last
For the times they are a changin'.'

I first heard those Bob Dylan lyrics at a Pete Seeger concert at the Melbourne Town Hall in 1964.

'Living well is the best revenge.'

The favourite maxim of Alexander Korda, the Hungarian who transformed the British film industry. The quote is now a best-seller on American T-shirts.

'Turn On, Tune In, Drop Out.'

The title of a lecture delivered by drug guru Timothy Leary in 1967.

'I cried all the way to the bank.'

Wladzou Valentino Liberace, born in 1919 and currently weeping over a multi-million law suit brought by a peevish youth.

'I'll make him an offer he can't refuse.'

That went straight into the language from Mario Puzo's *The Godfather*, published in 1969.

'Keep on truckin'.'

The catch-phrase of a cartoon character created by Robert Crumb.

'If I have to, I can do anything.
I am strong, I am invincible,
I am woman.'

The feminists' anthem, stirringly sung by Helen Reddy.

'The basic tenet of black consciousness is that the black man must reject all value systems that seek to make him a foreigner in the country of his birth and reduce his basic human dignity.'

A statement from Stephen Bantu Biko, who was born in 1946 and murdered by South African police in 1977.

'In a hierarchy, every employee tends to rise to his level of incompetence.'

A haunting proposition by Laurence Johnston Peter, otherwise known as the Peter Principle. First expounded in 1969.

'Like a bridge over troubled water,
I will lay me down.'

From a lyric by Paul Simon, written in 1969.

'When the President does it, that means it's not illegal.'

From Nixon's interview with David Frost, in 1977.

'All the way with LBJ.'

The joyful outburst that was to haunt Harold Holt.

'The medium is the message.'

One of the enigmatic aphorisms of the late Marshal Herbert McLuhan.

'You won't have Nixon to kick around any more, because, gentlemen, this is my last press conference.'

If only he'd meant it. Richard Milhous Nixon on 7 November 1962.

'I cannot and will not cut my conscience to fit this year's fashion.'

From Lillian Hellman's famous letter to the House UnAmerican Activities Committee (HUAC), 29 May 1952.

'Literary intellectuals at one pole — at the other, scientists. Between the two, a gulf of mutual incomprehension.'

It's 1959 and Sir Charles Percy Snow introduces the idea of the Two Cultures.

'Big Brother is watching you.'

Eric Blair, better known as George Orwell. From a novel about the future that will soon be set in the past.

'Well, back to the old drawing board.'

The caption for one of Peter Arno's *New Yorker* cartoons, showing a designer walking away from a plane wreck.

'Those who corrupt the public mind are just as evil as those who steal from the public purse.'

From a speech by Adlai Ewing Stevenson, delivered in September 1952. I can't forget that when Stevenson dropped dead on a London street in 1965, passers-by noticed that his right shoe had a hole in it.

'Here's looking at you, kid.'

Humphrey DeForest Bogart, playing in the classic film *Casablanca*, 1943.

'The past is a foreign country; they do things differently there.'

The compelling opening words of *The Go Between* by Leslie Poles Hartley.

'Either man is obsolete or war is.'

Richard Buckminster Fuller, speaking in 1970.

'Violence is necessary: it is as American as cherry pie.'

The black activist, Rap Brown, speaking in 1966.

'I have a dream that my four little children will one day live in a nation where they will not be judged by the colour of their skins, but by the content of their character.'

By a victim of that cherry-pie violence, Martin Luther King, assassinated in 1968.

'We are an intelligent species and the use of our intelligence quite properly gives us pleasure. In this respect the brain is like a muscle. When it is in use we feel very good. Understanding is joyous.'

From *Broca's Brain* by the admirable Carl Sagan.

'That's one small step for a man, one giant leap for mankind.'

Neil Alden Armstrong, presumably reading an idiot-sheet or auto-cue, as he lowered himself from the ladder to the lunar surface on 20 July 1969.

'I think that I shall never see
A billboard lovely as a tree.
Indeed unless the billboards fall
I'll never see a tree at all.'

Ogden Nash, 1902-1971

'What we've got here is a failure to communicate.'

One of those lines that leaps from a screenplay. In this case, Donn Pearce's *Cool Hand Luke* written in 1967.

'In spite of everything, I still believe that people are really good at heart.'

From the diary of a little girl who died at Auschwitz, Anne Frank, 1929-45.

'In the future, everyone will be world famous for 15 minutes.'

Written by Andy Warhol for the catalogue of his photographic exhibition in Stockholm in 1968.

'Power is the great aphrodisiac.'

From someone who ought to know — Henry Kissinger.

'A romantic fool, essentially a wind-bag full of rhetoric and metaphors.'

David Ben Gurion's unflattering assessment of Menachem Begin.

'Whether you like it or not, history is on our side. We will bury you.'

Nikita Krushchev, buried in 1971. A few days ago, Leonid Brezhnev was buried beside him.

'Include me out.'

Samuel Goldwyn, 1882-1977.

'Future Shock ... the shattering stress and disorientation that we induce in individuals by subjecting them to too much change in too short a time.'

Alvin Toffler, in 1970.

Oneupmanship.

A book title by Stephen Potter, 1900-69.

'I am the greatest.'

One of the best examples of oneupmanship, from Muhammad Ali, 1942-.

'Willie was a salesman. And for a salesman, there's no rock bottom to the life. He don't put a bolt to a nut, he don't tell you the law or give you medicine. He's a man way out there in the blue, riding on a smile and a shoe shine. And when they start not smiling back — that's an earthquake. And then you get yourself a couple of spots on your hat, and you're finished. Nobody dast blame this man. A salesman is got to dream, boy. It comes with the territory.'

The requiem from the stage play that affected me more than anything I'd ever seen, Arthur Miller's *Death of a Salesman*, written in 1949.

'The absurd is the essential concept and the first truth.'

Albert Camus, 1913-60.

'I saw the best minds of my generation destroyed by madness, starving, hysterical, naked.'

Alan Ginsberg, poet laureate to the beat generation, born in 1926.

'We, the peoples of the United Nations, determined to save succeeding generations from the scourge of war, which twice in our lifetime has brought untold sorrow to mankind, and to reaffirm faith and fundamental human rights, in the dignity and worth of the human person, in the equal rights of men and women and of all nations large and small . . .'

From the battered charter of the beleaguered United Nations, proclaimed in June 1945.

'Lord, won't you buy me a Mercedes Benz
My friends all drive Porsches
I must make amends.'

One of the minds of that generation destroyed by madness. Janis Joplin, an orphan of the storm of the 1960s, 1943-70.

'Do not go gentle into that good night
Old age should burn and rave at close of day.
Rage, rage against the dying of the light.'

From a poem by the late Dylan Thomas, written in 1952, the year before his death.

'There was only one catch and that was Catch-22, which specified that a concern for one's own safety in the face of dangers that were real and immediate was the process of a rational mind. Or was crazy and could be grounded. All he had to do was ask; and as soon as he did, he would no longer be crazy and he would have to fly missions ... If he flew them then he was crazy and didn't have to; but if he didn't want to he was sane and had to ... "That's some catch, that Catch-22," Yossarian observed. "It's the best there is," Doc Daneeka agreed.'

From Joseph Heller's magnificent book on the absurdities of war, *Catch-22*, first published in 1955 and still going strong.

'They give birth astride a grave, the light gleams an instant, then it's night once more.'

From Samuel Beckett's *Waiting for Godot*, probably the most important play of our century, first performed in 1952.

'A tramp, a gentleman, a poet, a dreamer, a lonely fellow, always hopeful of romance and adventure.'

Charlie (Sir Charles Spencer) Chaplin, 1889-1977, remembering his greatest character in his autobiography of 1964.

'I never forget a face, but in your case I'll make an exception.'

Groucho (Julius Henry) Marx, 1895-1977.

'So always look for the silver lining
And try to find the sunny side of life.'

Well, we're doing our best. From the lyrics of Sir Pelham Grenville Wodehouse, 1881-1975.

This compilation is the result of a fascinating literary experiment. Some years ago, on television, I saw Spike Milligan rolling a giant stone around to see if it gathered moss. In a similar spirit, I jumped off Princes Bridge into the whirling maelstrom of the Yarra, to see if my past would flash before my eyes. Instead, all those words rushed up to meet me and, as I sank for the third time, I heard a distant voice delivering the perfect, the *only* quotation with which to end. The last words on the last page of *The Great Gatsby* by Francis Scott Fitzgerald.

'So we beat on, boats against the current, borne back ceaselessly into the past.'

Someone to blame

Things are decidedly butcher's. The economy is flat, weary, stale and unprofitable ... the environment is knackered ... nuclear war is imminent ... it's the non-ratings period for television ... and unemployment is spreading like herpes. And to top it all off, the drought has us sewing stamps on envelopes.

For once society is united. We all agree that things couldn't be worse but certainly will be. Moved you, seconded me, passed unanimously. What we *don't* agree on is whom or what to blame.

And having someone or something to blame is *imperative*. Unless you can point the finger, pass the buck, cast the first stone, accuse, charge or impute, you feel so ... bloody frustrated. The one pleasure of living in difficult times is *screaming* at somebody.

'This is the excellent foppery of the world that, when we are sick in fortune — often of surfeit of our own behaviour — we make guilty of our disasters the Sun, the Moon and the stars.' Shakespeare, in *King Lear*. Yet here we are with our kids on drugs, our ferns going brown and the term 'Commonwealth' taking on an aspect of political satire ... and it's hard to know whom to abuse.

Take last weekend's *Age*. When interviewed in depth, the voters of Flinders seemed disinclined to blame anybody in particular for the mess we're in. It seems we're victims of a generalised malaise. Like planetary mumps.

Well, it just won't do. Somebody or something *has* to be responsible. We have to find a scapegoat. Impeachment, indictment, *denouncement* is essential to community health. It's a sort of group therapy for dark and difficult times. So here goes with a list of alternatives, people and things that have proved to be blameworthy over the years and the centuries.

1. *The Devil*. Also marketed under the alternative brand-names of Satan, Lucifer, Beelzebub, the Prince of Darkness, Mephistopheles and His Satanic Majesty. A *very* popular target for communal hostility, used by the Christian Church for almost 2,000 years. Unfortunately the Devil has become a bit passé — as a result of improved education and trendy theology. He was also somewhat subverted by Sigmund Freud's notion of the subconscious. Yet with ancient superstition making a comeback (e.g. astrology, Nostradamus and Friedmanite economic theories) the Devil *could* be ready for a Second Coming. If you're interested in checking out the Tempter, the Archfiend, the Angel of the Bottomless Pit, I suggest you audition the electronic evangelists screened by our TV networks on Sabbath mornings.

2. *Gough Whitlam.* For many people, Whitlam superseded the Devil in 1972. Even today, many Liberals wear garlic around their necks and make the sign of the cross whenever his name is mentioned. For almost ten years anything and everything wrong with Australia has been blamed on Gough who, allegedly, took a perfectly idyllic country and

turned it into a sort of Bolshies' pig trough. Life-long conservatives swept up in the euphoria are still trying to live down their 'It's Time' lapse by beating themselves with nettles. However it's getting harder and harder to blame Whitlam as he recedes into ancient history, like the FJ Holden, Johnny O'Keefe and the Darrod's Wheel.

3. *Bomb Tests*. You could blame a lot of things on them in the 1950s, like Strontium 90 in the milk and the strange weather we were having. 'It's them bomb tests', people would mutter ominously. However in recent years they seem to have run out of puff.

4. *The Media*. Just as the poor workman blames his tools, a poor society blames its media. The messenger is blamed for the message. Politicians are particularly anxious to curse the press for their troubles — which seems only fair when the press are forever blaming the politicians. On balance, the media has much to answer for — including gloomy headlines, mediocre prose, pompous film critics and too many SABA commercials.

5. *Witches*. For centuries, a wide variety of social and personal ills could be blamed on witchcraft and sorcery. Male chauvinism reached unprecedented heights as tens of thousands of women were publicly barbecued. Although the burning of crones was a great boost to community morale, any resurgence is likely to be opposed by the feminists.

6. *Dole Bludgers*. These despicable creatures were the human counterpart to white ants, destroying society from the inside. Sadly, the dole bludger seems destined to become an anachronism, like 'Juvenile Delinquent' and 'Bohemian' for, according to economic calculations, western societies will soon be so broke that there'll be no dole to bludge.

7. *Foreign Ownership*. During the 1960s that was clearly the problem. All those Wall Street swine robbing Australia of its birthright. Sucking us dry. Digging the ground from beneath our feet. If we kicked the bastards out, we'd all be

rolling in it. Like bomb tests, foreign ownership no longer arouses strong passions. This is because foreign ownership, like bomb tests, is now conducted underground.

8 *Jews*. For centuries, Christendom has used the Jew interchangeably with the Devil. They were too clever by half, owned everything and were involved in a global conspiracy of awesome dimensions. Therefore Christians were entitled to shove them into ghettos, conduct pogroms against them and exclude them from the Melbourne Club. However, after the excesses of the Third Reich, anti-Semitism became briefly unfashionable. So much so that after a mere 2,000 years the Vatican recently absolved the Jews from the collective guilt of killing Christ. Now anti-Semitism is making a big comeback in Moscow, Paris, Berlin and just about everywhere. Once again Jews are soaring up the Hate Parade.

9 *Arabs*. For a brief time in the 1970s, Arabs replaced Jews as the focus of global hostility. After all, they'd had the audacity to want money for their oil. To make matters worse, these extras from the Desert Song were traffic-jamming Regent Street in their Rolls Royces. However, in recent years Arabs have posed a declining threat as they've been so busy killing each other.

10 *Parents*. During the 1950s and the 1960s parents could be blamed for just about everything. As teenagers we could point to the way they'd stuffed the world up. We could complain about the mess we'd inherited. We could point the finger of scorn at their wretched, rotten values and so forth. Trouble is we're now parents ourselves.

11 *Kids*. As we know, these are ungrateful, undisciplined, rotten little swine. They are insubordinate, unkempt and ungrateful. Think of everything we've done for them. Consider all the sacrifices we've made! Unfortunately it's hard to sustain such sanctimonious attitudes when the future looks so crook. Suddenly the best years of your life are leaving much to be desired. Like jobs, for example.

12 *Malcolm Fraser*. Like Gough, Malcolm could be held personally responsible. Indeed, he seemed to like it that way. Such was his hauteur and superciliousness that he seemed determined to provoke community anger. Thou shalt have no other politician before me, for I am angry god. Now we realise that he's just a human being with sciatica, another politician who couldn't cope. God help us, there were even times when I felt vaguely sorry for him.

13 *Abos*. People of dusky pigmentation are still the focus of hostility in the Northern Territory and Queensland. 'They get the best of everything', people complain. Like leprosy and trauchoma.

14 *Vietnamese*. A popular new target in our larger cities. 'We're being over-run by the slant-eyed bastards', is this latest variation of the Yellow Peril. Why don't we send them back to their own country, along with all the wogs and whingeing Pommies?

15 *Commies*. Very popular in the Menzies and McCarthy era. Although Ronald Reagan still markets them as the anti-Christ, they no longer strike much terror in the antipodes. This is because hostilities were reduced by Michael Edgley bringing out the Moscow Circus and because when we saw John Halfpenny on the telly, he didn't seem such a bad bloke.

16 *The Permissive Society*. This has made up a lot of ground in recent years, thanks to the Festival of Light and the Moral Majority. While we shouldn't criticise God, it's clear that He made a very serious error in (a) inventing sex, and (b) making it enjoyable. Having seen the error of His ways (largely thanks to the splendid efforts of the Reverend Fred Nile) the Almighty is now turning the tide by introducing new and more virulent strains of VD. By waging biological war against concupiscence there may just be time to salvage what's left of western civilisation.

17 *The Microchip*. If it wasn't for that, everything would be lovely. It's computers that are really at fault, rendering the

human being obsolete. They can be blamed for soaring unemployment, for social alienation, for a world in which people will soon be strangers. Computers sap the ability of our politicians to make decisions and make us all victims of 'technological determinism'. In the face of their inexorable advance, we are rendered impotent. Worse still, their incomprehensibility makes one feel stupid.

18 *Trade Unions*. Congregating together in a gloomy building in Lygon Street, unions are a good thing that has become a bad thing. Most social problems are, quite clearly, their fault. If they only had the commonsense to abandon everything they'd fought to achieve (like the right to strike, minimum wages and decent working conditions) everything would be all right. Trade union officials are the bogeymen of the 1980s. That is, unless they're *Polish* trade union officials who are selfless and heroic.

19 *Drugs, Metrication and Decimal Currency*. Along with chemicals in our food and television, these modern phenomena can be blamed for a wide variety of social ills. Recommended antidotes include stone-ground flour, free range eggs and voting Australian Democrat.

20 *Evil Spirits*. For thousands of years, a popular target of communal hostility. Still popular among the more exotic migrant groups in our inner suburbs. The Health Department fears that evil spirits are being introduced into Australia by tourists returning from Bali. They have recommended additional spraying in in-coming jets.

All in all, that's a fairly listless, lacklustre list. With the possible exception of Union Bashing, it's a fairly unexciting collection. And think of it. If we can't blame the Devil, Gough, Bomb Tests, the Media, Witches, Dole Bludgers, Foreign Ownership, Jews, Arabs, Parents, Kids, Malcolm Fraser, Abos, Vietnamese, Commies, the Permissive Society, the Microchip, Drugs, Metrication or Decimal Currency for our troubles, it looks as though we'll have to face the music and the awful prospect of . . . blaming ourselves.

Expressing déjà views

Was tomorrow the same as yesterday will be?
Do you believe in preincarnation?
Is this where we came in?
In other words, is the march of time caught in a revolving door?

I raise this confusion of chronology because Malcolm Muggeridge tells me we're reliving those roller coaster years, the 1920s and 1930s. Far from being unprecedented, our experiences of permissiveness and financial catastrophe are, in effect, a video replay.

And Muggers may well be right. Economic history certainly does seem to be repeating itself, as are our politicians, businessmen and bureaucrats. My researches show that they are echoing the same opinions and singing the same songs. Expressing déjà views.

For the evidence, read the old newspapers preserved beneath the kitchen lino; beginning on 4 December 1928, with the following message from President Calvin Coolidge.

'No Congress of the United States ever assembled, on surveying the state of the union, has met with a more pleasing prospect ... in the domestic field there is tranquility and contentment, harmonious relations between management and wage earner, freedom from industrial strife, and the highest record of years of prosperity.'

That's the sort of political positivism our politicians are forever employing in policy speeches. As Charles Curtis, a Vice Presidential candidate in 1928, put it 'the only issue in this campaign is the continued prosperity of the American people'.

With the US poised on the brink of disaster, as it is today, what were its national leaders saying? A writer, after eating breakfast with candidate Hoover: 'The kind of prosperity which Mr Hoover is so earnestly seeking to promote and perpetuate

... is widely diffused prosperity, percolating through all sections of the country, benefiting the people, adding to the contents not merely of their pocket books, but of their lives'. His words were echoed by economist Irving Fisher. 'Mr Hoover is a practical economist and one to whom is due more largely than to any other one man the improvement in our prosperity. Mr Hoover knows as few men do the terrible evils in inflation and deflation.'

Roger W. Batterson, yet another economist, agreed. 'If Smith should be elected with a Democratic Congress, we are almost certain to have a resultant business depression in 1929. The election of Hoover and a Republican Congress should result in continued prosperity.'

From Charles Curtis, another Vice Presidential hopeful, 'Stick to the full dinner pail! You have been enjoying Republican prosperity. If you want to continue the prosperity of the administrations of Calvin Coolidge, vote for Hoover!'

If all that sounds familiar to electors of the 1980s so do the homilies from Herbert H. himself. 'Employment in the sense of distress is widely disappearing ... we in America today are nearer to the final triumph over poverty than ever before in the history of any land ... were it not for sound government policies and leadership, employment conditions in America today would be similar to those existing in many other parts of the world ... the outlook is for the greatest era of commercial expansion in history.'

And now, a chorus of contemporary voices from that best-of-all possible worlds.

'There will be no interruption of our present prosperity.'

Myron E. Forbes, President, Pearce-Arrow motor car company, 1 January 1928

'I cannot help but raise a dissenting voice to statements that we are simply living in a fool's paradise, and that prosperity in this country must necessarily diminish and recede in the future.'

E.H. Simmons, President, New York Stock Exchange, 12 January 1928

'We are only at the beginning of a period that will go down in history as the golden age.'

Irving T. Bush, President, Bush Terminal Co., 15 November 1928

'Suggestions that the wiping out of paper profits will reduce the country's real purchasing power seem far fetched.'

Wall Street Journal, 26 October 1929

'We probably have three more years of prosperity ahead of us before we enter the cyclic tail-spin which has occurred in the 11th year of each of the four great previous periods of commercial prosperity.'

Stuart Chase, columnist, 1 November 1929

'Comparatively few people are touched by this crash.'

Julius Rosenwals, Sears Roebuck & Co., 9 November 1929

'To my mind the situation should go no further.'

Jessie Livermore, Financier, 13 November 1929

'It looks as if industry will have to begin scraping around to get employees instead of laying off anybody.'

Alexander Legge, Chairman, Federal Farm Board, 22 November 1929

'There are no great failures, nor are there likely to be.'

Monthly Review, National City Bank, 2 December 1929

'Some reassuring utterance by the President of the United States would do much to restore the confidence of the public.'

William Randolph Hearst, 29 November 1929

'Any lack of confidence in the economic future or the basic strength of business in the United States is foolish.'

President Hoover, 29 November 1929

1930 was the year of positive thinking. Positive thinking, but negative results.

8 March 1930. 'President Hoover predicted today that the worst effect of the crash upon unemployment will have been passed during the next 60 days.'

1 May 1930. President Hoover said today that 'While the crash took place only 6 months ago I am convinced that we have now passed the worst and with continued unity of effort shall rapidly recover'.

18 October 1931. 'The depression has been deepened by events from abroad', said the President in a radio address, 'which are beyond the control of either our citizens or our Government ... economic depression can't be cured by legislative action or Executive pronouncement'.

In an attempt to bolster consumer confidence, John D. Rockefeller Snr made the following announcement: 'Believing that fundamental conditions of the country are sound ... my son and I have for some days been purchasing sound common stocks. We are continuing and will continue our purchases in substantial amounts at levels which we believe represent sound investment values'.

Sadly, those sound common stocks continued to plummet. Chrysler dropped from 35 to 11, DuPont from 129 to 53, General Motors from 50 to 22, Montgomery Ward from 66 to 8, and Sears Roebuck from 108 to 31. Meanwhile the value of US Steel and Western Union were slashed by two-thirds.

Andrew W. Mellon, Secretary of the Treasury, was undaunted. 'There is no cause for worry. The high tide of prosperity will continue.' Unfased by calamity he trumpeted 'the government's businesses and sound condition'. And a year later his New Year message was 'I see nothing in the present situation that is either menacing or warrants pessimism'.

Sixteen months later Mellon addressed the Congress of the International Chamber of Commerce. 'In this country there has been a concerted and determined effort on behalf of both Government and business not only to prevent any reduction in wages, but to keep the maximum number of men employed and thereby to increase consumption. The standard of living must be maintained at all costs.'

Well, not quite *all* costs. Shortly thereafter, the Aluminium Company of America and its subsidiaries (all controlled by the Mellon family) reduced the wages of employees by 10 per cent.

Meanwhile, in the boardroom of Bethlehem Steel, Chairman Charles M. Schwab was bullish. 'I do not feel there is any danger to the public in the present situation. As long as the people remain enthusiastic and interested the market will hold up.' (5 March 1929)

'In my long association with the steel industry, I have never known it to enjoy a greater stability or more promising outlook than it does today.' (25 October 1929)

'Never before has American business been as firmly entrenched for prosperity as it is today. Steel's three biggest customers, the automobile, railway and building industries, seem to me to justify a healthy outlook. The nation will prosper.' (10 December 1929)

A year later, Schwab was still undismayed. 'Looking to the future I see in the further acceleration of science continuous jobs for our workers. Science will cure unemployment.'

And while bankrupts did swallow-dives out of their office windows, Schwab's mates insisted that everything was hunky-dory. It wasn't so much a case of happy days being here again —

they hadn't even departed. Consider the following VIP Vox Pop . . .

'Now everyone will get to work.'

Alfred P. Sloan, President, General Motors

'Happily we have now turned our backs upon the events of this unfortunate episode.'

Paul M. Warberg, Federal Reserve Board

'Following my visits to a number of cities in the last 60 days, I have reached the conclusion that this is going to be a good business year.'

D.G. Biechler, Frigidaire

'By next October business will be back to an activity actually higher than last year and much higher than the preceding years.'

Dr Rupert S. Tucker, Economist, American Foundation Corp.

'There is no reason for people to get their wind up.'

The Governor of the Bank of England

'The economic maladjustment of this period will without a doubt be ironed out before many months have elapsed.'

Sir Joseph Stamp, Bank of England

'The economic maladjustment of this period will without a doubt be ironed out before many months have elapsed.'

Dr Randolph Burgess, Federal Reserve Bank of New York

> 'Prophecy is a vain thing and I have no wish to join the ranks of the prophets, but I believe that we have turned the corner.'

P.E. Crowley, President, New York Central Railroad

> 'It will surprise many to know how good business is right now.'

Arthur Reynolds, Chicago banker

> 'The general slump in business in my opinion has been greatly exaggerated.'

R.W. Woodruff, President, Coca-Cola Company

> 'If we all buckled down to our jobs, prosperity will be back again before we realise it.'

Adolf Zukor, motion picture producer

> 'The worst is over without a doubt.'

James J. Davis, Secretary of Labor

> 'Judged by historic precedences, we have now reached low ebb.'

Resolution of Bankers Association

And let Alfred P. Sloan of G-M utter some famous last words:

> 'I can see no reason why 1931 should not be an *extremely* good year.'

Wasn't it Lord Nelson who, holding a telescope to his blind eye, said that 'I can't see any ships with holes in them'? In 1930, as in 1982, an awful lot of Lord Nelsons were holding telescopes to blind eyes.

The world is crawling with Harry Limes

A few streets away the 18-year-old son of two friends is found dead from an overdose of heroin. Though tragedy and justice are always strangers, this death is numbing in its cruelty.

Wondering how a thing like this could happen, I find my thoughts drifting to a scene in a film I'd watched, yet again, the night before. It was *The Third Man* in which Graham Greene wrote a sort of policy speech for the 20th century. You'll recall that Harry Lime has been selling adulterated penicillin on the black market, filling a terminal ward with his victims, largely children. Far from apologising for his profiteering, he takes a friend on a ride above the city, in Vienna's giant ferris wheel. Lime points to the people far, far below, dismissing them as just 'black dots'. Contemptuous of his friend's moral outrage, he asks 'And if you were offered £20,000 for every black dot that disappeared?' The mocking, ironic Mr Lime has no trouble with that equation.

These days the world is crawling with Harry Limes who soar above the world in their ferris wheels of indifference, seeing everyone as black dots, fair game for their murderous transactions.

It's said that some very prominent Australians are involved in the heroin racket. Not that the Harry Limes stop with drugs — they've missiles and napalm and nuclear weapons in their sample bags. For in the final analysis, there's no moral difference between one black dot and a million.

They approach the business of destruction, whether of an individual or of a people, with the same serenity. The businessmen who killed my friends' son rise above us, so rich and powerful that they're beyond the reach of a legal system that, by all accounts, they've thoroughly corrupted.

But just as the arms dealers don't actually fire the missiles, the powerful men who land heroin in Australia by the containerful didn't actually place the syringe in the boy's hand. So why did the bright, intelligent son of two fine people die? We sit and talk about that. It's hard to see whether there are reasons for it or whether it comes about through *lack* of reasons. Finally it isn't a question of reasons but of confusions.

When we were kids, an act of defiance (of parents, teachers, or the State) was a duck's bum haircut, a cigarette behind the shelter shed, or a slashed train seat. And we coped with our existential anxieties, particularly of the Cold War, with the nonsense of Spike Milligan. The Goons were, of course, group therapists to an entire generation. These days, it seems, a kid needs more than a surreptitious cigarette and the famous Eccles. Nonsense has escalated to horror-filled absurdity, to the sort of nihilism that needs a needle.

While we sat together, remembering the boy, another friend arrived. A social worker, she reminded us that as kids we could drift from job to job. We could have ten jobs, twenty. Our parents would criticise us for lack of discipline but finally we'd find a job that we could live with and our lives would start to have a focus. Well, few of today's kids can even get that first job. At the same time, it must be admitted that, for some of the brightest and most alienated, there'd never be a job that made sense.

The boy had laughed at any suggestion of Odyssey, rejecting every attempt to help him. He'd mocked psychiatrists, mimicking their voices and arguments. In that sense he was typical of the brighter, cleverer addict. And not just the addict — the brighter, cleverer kid. For the children of the 20th century, of the age of media, have more sophistication and knowledge than any kids in history. More knowledge but less wisdom.

There was a time, not so long ago, when time moved slowly, when the mood changes of society were not so mercurial. Now we're bombarded by radio, by the ever-changing kaleidoscope of television, by the floodtide of impressions that fragment our experiences. Turn on the telly and you're wrenched from the Falkland Islands to Big M to the bombing of the Lebanon to Buy a Toyota to see *Mad Max* to the Lotto numbers in as many seconds. And television is only one of the countless inputs that crowd and cloud the senses. In this discontinuity lie the seeds to disaster. For while we *think* that we're informed, we are really bewildered.

Our kids grow up street wise but world foolish. You saw the phenomenon very clearly in the Beatles who were exhilarating in their cheek and audacity. Yet for all their savvy, they fell prey to the media that made them and prey, too, to giggling gurus, drugs and half-baked ideas.

Or no ideas at all. Sometimes the kids seem to abandon themselves to randomness. As I walked up the hall with the boy's father, I looked inside his son's bedroom and noticed a paperback lying open on the floor. It was a novel that trendies embraced some ten years ago called *The Dice Man*. The hero was a bloke who'd given up making decisions. Instead he voted to live his life as a gambler, simply listing the options in any situation and tossing the dice. In a sense, that's what the boy had done with his young life. Gambled it away, thrown it away. A sacrifice made all the more poignant by his qualities and intelligence.

Ten years ago I wrote urging that addicts be registered, as they are in Britain. That their drugs be provided free. I can remember being astonished by the sight of addicts coming out of the subway at Piccadilly, waiting to have their prescriptions filled at Boots. But two things were immediately apparent. First, this enlightened law had done much to keep the Harry Limes out of the drug business. (If the addicts could get it for nothing, it was hard to make a quid.) And secondly, the idea of licensing junkies somehow destroyed the warped glamour that surrounds the business. If your suicidal protests lead to a form of official registration rather than howling police sirens and over-dramatised notoriety, then the *elitism* of the addict begins to disintegrate.

I'm not saying that Britain doesn't have a drug problem but it's nothing like as severe as the spectre that stalks countries like America and Australia. Surely it's not too late for Australia to adopt this pragmatic, life-saving policy.

The next day I talked to a friend who lectures at a tech. where the only place you can't buy drugs is at the tuck shop. 'The kids will do anything, take anything. Grog, pills, LSD, cocaine, whatever they can get. In almost any combination. They'll stay up half the night doing terrible things to themselves. And they'll be back at school next morning in fairly good shape. Because they're young and healthy, they're resilient. So they can't see that they're doing themselves any harm. They simply don't believe it's going to kill them. Because retribution is postponed, it can be ignored. And by the time they do realise what it's doing to them, it's too late.'

But retribution must not be postponed for the Harry Limes of the heroin trade. As in the final scenes of a film that became an allegory, they must be hunted down in the sewers where they belong.

Death, or my hobby hearse

Australia's columnists have pet subjects to which they repeatedly, even obsessively return. Thus Bob Santamaria seems a bit peeved about Communism, David McNicoll wants more sympathy for the Boer and Max Harris wants us to recognise the extraordinary significance of Max Harris. And for me, writing has been a sort of death watch. Death is, if you will, my hobby hearse and in over twenty years I've written a long cortège of columns on society's unwillingness to confront it. I see the most pathological censorship of sexual matters as a symptom of a more profound taboo — the Great Hush-Up that surrounds croaking, bucket-kicking, expiring and giving up the ghost. Not to mention shuffling off this mortal coil.

And while I've been addressing this topic in deadly earnest, trying to tear the shroud away, to get death's skeleton out of society's cupboard, a lady in America has been doing much the same. Only more so. Dr Kubler-Ross has toured the world making lectures and promoting a shelf full of books on the significance of snuffing, and how we mortals might come to terms with it. Without employing the death-denying nonsense of religion and without burying the subject, along with our dead, in euphemisms — like 'passing on' and 'resting in peace'. As a result of a missionary zeal, the study of death, Thanatology, became trendy in universities across America.

A great success on the late Bob Moore's *Monday Conference*, Dr Kubler-Ross recently returned to the ABC in a very sympathetic documentary that showed her jet-setting from hospital to hospice, bringing tranquillity to the terminally ill. Her commonsense and sympathy could be seen helping both the dying and their next of kin. She explained how it had all begun, for her, when visiting the Third Reich's death camps where young children, while queueing for the gas chambers, had drawn butterflies on the walls. It was an admirable programme about an interesting woman, the humanist counterpart to Sister Theresa.

But there's one small problem. About eighteen months ago Kubler-Ross reneged. She completely changed her beliefs or, if you prefer, her disbeliefs. To put the programme to air without telling the viewers of this transformation was as sloppy as running a biographical film on Sister Theresa *without* revealing that she'd recently kicked the habit and become a go-go dancer.

It is my sad duty to report that Kubler-Ross is now a member of one of the looniest of California's religious cults whose adherents claim to have sexual intercourse with ghosts. Moreover the good doctor now insists that she has 'mathematical evidence', whatever that might be, of life after death. What next? Will Bill Hartley denounce Gaddafi and become a CIA operative? Will Bob Hawke go Gay?

Yet to watch the documentary on Kubler-Ross, made before her conversion, was to see the symptoms. Here was a classic case of the zealot changing sides. In the 1950s a number of prominent communist intellectuals suddenly metamorphosed into mystics or ultra-conservatives. Recently the American press reported, with open-mouthed astonishment, that the ultra radical Jerry Rubin was now working as an investment consultant on Wall Street. But in a sense these apparent turn-arounds are examples of unswerving consistency.

If a political extremist of the Left finishes up an extremist of the Right, the consistency is in his political extremism. When a rabid anti-Catholic goes on a pilgrimage to Lourdes, the consistency lies in his fascination with the Church. When a prominent crusader against homosexuality is arrested loitering in a public loo, one recalls the Shakespearean observation 'Methinks he doth protest too much'.

Just as our anti-porn crusaders are sometimes a little *too* interested in porn, Kubler-Ross was a little too interested in death. Watching her sitting at death beds, helping the doomed compose themselves, you realise that it was *she* who was being helped. In teaching those people to die with dignity, she was seeking to learn how to live. To live with less fear. And I was reminded of my involvement, a couple of years back, with one of those telephone volunteer services, where would-be suicides ring for a chat. Asked to recruit more volunteers, I was told that such services tend to attract the disturbed, that many of the people giving advice to the desperate are perilously unstable themselves. But in the course of their time as volunteers, in helping solve the problems of others, they begin to solve their own problems so that when they leave the service they're far, far stronger personalities.

This is clearly what Kubler-Ross was doing, albeit unconsciously. In the terminal wards she was trying to control her own terrors. It was a case of 'physician, heal thyself'.

But in the end Kubler-Ross's nightmares were too intense and she couldn't heed her own advice. Turning against her teachings, she renounced her professed philosophies and capitulated to the sorts of superstitions she'd been denouncing for decades.

It's as well to remember this phenomenon when listening to the missionaries, whether they're propounding Methodism or Monetarism. In my experience, the more unshakeable the utterance, the greater the doubt. Inside many an arrogant attitude, there's an anxiety trying to escape.

Bonsai'd bibles and other condensations

While Nestlés condense milk, the Reader's Digest condense literature. Over the years they've taken out the self-indulgent bits from countless novels, invisibly mended the prose, and printed the plots. Freed of descriptive passages and redundant adjectives, this filleted fiction has enjoyed widespread popularity. Well, it's one up from claiming familiarity with a novel as a result of reading the blurb on the dust jacket.

Needless to say, the Digest has taken a lot of flak over this practice. There are people who've accused them of literary loutishness, verbal vandalism, bibliographic blasphemy. But the Digest sails on, cocking its snoot at the pedants. And perhaps it attempts to make amends by publishing its 'It pays to increase your word power' feature. Just to show that its final aim is not the destruction of literacy.

I understand that the Digest is now run by an Australian, Frank Devine. Given that the Digest oft claims divine inspiration, his promotion from the colonies was probably inevitable. And it's under Frank's leadership that the Digest has embarked upon its most audacious condensation... the *Reader's Digest Condensed Bible*. Mind you, they can't condense the Bible enough for me. However I do like the Bible when it's condensed into Cecil B. deMille movies and am enthralled to think that our very own Bruce Beresford is working on the hunk of the Old Testament concerning King David. It's about time the Old Testament was energetically ockerised and given a touch of the Bazzas.

I distinctly remember from Sunday School that the Bible is written in an archaic code that our betters tell us is great literature. Apart from the few dirty bits in the Song of Solomon, me and my mates at Eltham High couldn't make much sense of it at all so I'm not going to criticise the Digest for doing a bit of judicious trimming. But it seems that their bonsai'd bible has outraged the entire Christian world, creating the one truly effective wave of ecumenism this century. Suddenly the Southern Fundamentalists are united with the loftiest biblical scholars who dote on the St James version. Suddenly the Vatican has joined hands with the Episcopalians who, in turn, are shoulder to shoulder with the Methodists. If the Bible is the word of God, what right has Frank Devine got to fiddle with it? As far as Christianity is concerned, every comma and consonant, every vowel and verb is sacred and nobody but the Almighty can apply the blue pencil.

Given an increasingly crowded planet, surely condensations are essential. I understand that even the Japanese are growing taller as a result of improved nutrition — at a time when it would make much more sense if we all grew smaller. It's time to emulate the pygmies, those condensed people. And who better than the Japanese to show us the way? They have, after all, condensed the car and the radio very effectively indeed.

Let us look, therefore, for other examples of condensations.

The Jennings' triple-fronted brick veneer is, arguably, a condensed Windsor Castle. John Howard failed to win the leadership of the Liberal Party because he was seen by many as a condensed Malcolm Fraser. Vitamin pills are condensed meals, Toulouse Lautrec was a condensed painter and the Young Liberals have condensed IQs.

New Zealand is the Reader's Digest's condensed Australia, just as Little Patti is the condensed Debbie Reynolds who, herself, was a condensed Doris Day.

Omo commercials are condensed soap operas. Children are condensed adults and goldfish are condensed whales.

The Daihatsu is a condensed Datsun and a critic is a *very* condensed artist. A lizard is a condensed dinosaur, and the Church of England is condensed Catholicism.

The devalued Australian dollar is a condensed currency, a miniature is a condensed mural, and Max Phipps was a sadly condensed Whitlam. The wallaby is a condensed kangaroo and a trailer is a condensed movie. If readers can think of other examples of condensation, I'll print them with appropriate reward.

But back to the *Reader's Digest Condensed Bible*. I understand that Frank Devine used his Devine authority to condense the Ten Commandments down to a more manageable six. References to neighbour's oxes were deleted as anachronistic, along with a few old-fashioned admonishments to prudery.

The Creation was also condensed down to three days which means that Christians who embrace the Digest version will have to have their Sundays on Thursdays.

It's time we did something

On 6 April 1981 Ian Melrose Pattison was to appear in the Dandenong Magistrates Court in relation to charges of indecent assault. Found guilty, he would be sentenced to six months.

The night before, Pattison celebrated his final hours of freedom by abducting, raping, torturing and mutilating a young woman. From being the victim of one of the worst crimes in Australian history she has now become a victim of a great social injustice. For after a year of unimaginable suffering, the Crimes Compensation Tribunal awarded her just $7,500. The sort of petty cash that someone gets for losing a fingertip in an industrial accident or for a mild case of whiplash.

A pleasant faced woman of thirty-two years, Valerie is also remarkably courageous. Today her story, in her own words . . .

'It was late when I finished work and walked to my car. A man approached me and mumbled something. I didn't understand and said "I beg your pardon?" He said he wanted money. I said "Here's my bag — take the whole lot". That's when I saw the knife. He jabbed me with it and motioned me into Victoria Street and behind some flats. He said "Don't speak or I'll kill you. Do as I tell you. Lie down while I tie you up and leave you here. Otherwise you're going to be history."

'It was like something out of a fantasy. My biggest mistake was letting him tie me up, believing that he'd go away. Instead he gagged me, put a hood on my face and interfered with me. He picked me up and threw me in the boot of a car and when I kicked at him, punched me.

'Then he drove away and I thought "I can't die because there are so many things I have to do . . ." There was a man I loved very much and I had hopes for a future with him so I just couldn't die.

'He drove for over an hour and I managed to untie myself.

What was I going to do when he stopped the car and opened it? Is he going to kill me? Has he got a gun? Is he going to set the car on fire, because I could smell petrol? What am I going to do if he takes me into his house? Into the bush? What am I going to do if I can get out of this boot? Or if he leaves me in the boot to rot?

'I found a jack and thought when he opens the boot, I'll use this. But if I hit him, I'm going to keep on hitting him, and could kill him. Then how will I prove that it was self-defence? How am I going to prove that I was tied and thrown into the boot? That I had never known the bloke before? That I'd never even seen him before in my life? How can I prove these things if I kill him? My name splashed all over the papers, all over the country. What about my life then?

'As it turned out, he opened the boot very, very slowly, the knife in his right hand. He got a shock seeing me untied holding the jack and said "What are you going to do now?" I said "I'm going to let you have it, and I mean it. Let me go, you've got the money. Let me go. Leave me alone."

'He said "I'm not going to hurt you, I just want to have intercourse with you."

'I started to fight. Instead of stabbing me with the knife, he began punching. I punched him back, tried to hurt him back, but he went wild. He said "I'll pay you back — you shouldn't have done that. You really hurt me." Then he tied my hands and said "I won't kill you, I promise I won't kill you. I'll leave you here in the bush."

'It wasn't just intercourse. This is what most people don't understand. You think rape means intercourse and that's the end of it. But intercourse is nothing. He mutilated my body over and over again with the knife. Through the whole ordeal I wasn't allowed to speak. He said to me "If you want to say something, ask permission". If I didn't, he'd punch me or cut me with the knife. And I would plead "Don't", but he would do it even more. I realised he was a sadist and didn't want him to know I was feeling pain in any way. I pretended that I wasn't there. My body was there, but my mind wasn't. If I'd let my mind accept the situation today I'd be in an asylum. It wasn't just a matter of being sexually assaulted, it was all the things he did to me. And the pain.

'I remember trying to analyse what kind of man he was. I would ask his permission to speak. I would say to him "Why are you doing this? You're a young man. You can get a woman anywhere you like." He said that he hated women, that they're all bitches and that they should all pay for it. Pay for what? He told me to shut up. It went on and on.

'At one stage I tried to get his sympathy. I said to him I've got a little boy and my husband left me and I have to support the boy. That's why I'm working at night. He said "Why don't you work in a massage parlour? You'd make a lot of money." I told him that some people are brought up differently. Then I told him I was pregnant and begged him not to hurt me too much. But he seemed to enjoy the fact that I was pregnant. He said "I'll look after you and the kid." He said he wanted to belong to someone, that he wanted to be loved.

'I asked him why he didn't go to a massage parlour. He said "Why should I fork out money for something that I can get for free? After all, those girls wouldn't cop what you're copping now, would they?" They were his exact words.

'He said "Of all the women I could have picked on I had to pick on you." Because through the whole ordeal I wouldn't show pain. When he chopped my nipple off he said to me "Why don't you scream. Why don't you say something?" I said you can do what you want with my body, but you can't have my soul.

'He said "I will leave you here, I'll tie you up and make sure you can't get away." He tied my wrists very hard again, my feet, right across my arms, right along my whole body. Then he joined a rope from my neck to my hands and feet. He took his knife and said "I could kill you now. I could even hang you, I could do what I want."

'I asked him to do me a favour before I died. I wasn't going to die in fear. I was going to die with dignity and pride. So he said "What do you want me to do?" I said, take the blindfold off my face and look me straight in the eye when you're doing it. He said "I can't do that. And I can't kill you."

'He started to cry then and said he was sorry for what he'd done. He then talked of the shack in the hills where he was going to take me, where he'd spend three weeks with me. "I'll look after you, I'll bring food and I'll really look after you." And he left me to look for the hut!

'The only things I could move were my chin, shoulders and toes. I felt I was on the slope of a hill so I moved my body to roll down. I said to myself "God, you've got me in this situation. He mustn't find me again." I relaxed for a few minutes and listened to the traffic in the background. In which direction was it coming from? There were two roads but which one was closer? I felt my body cooling and knew I would be stiff soon, and unable to move at all. I used my chin to push myself against the earth. And with my knees.

'In the next three hours, I felt fear three times. The first was when I fell into mud and gravel. The second was when I was stuck between a tree and a rock. My whole body was stuck between the tree and the rock and I literally couldn't move. That's when I broke down and cried. But I pushed myself forward, inch by inch and was able to get back on my knees and crawl. The third time I felt fear was when I heard a rustle in the grass behind me. I thought he was slowly walking behind me. I turned around on several occasions and said "Why don't you leave me alone?" But it wasn't him. I was towing along this rag, a part of my clothing that was caught in the ropes. And when I went through three barbed wire fences, I was terrified I was going around in circles.

'At the third barbed wire fence I managed to tear away part of the hood. I was frightened I'd tear out my eye. But I hooked the hood on a piece of wire and pushed myself against it. The hood opened and I could see daylight, could see the traffic straight ahead. I was totally exhausted. I could feel so much pain and saw the gash in my breast and there were flies everywhere. I couldn't do anything about it.

'I tried to scream out to the traffic — "Help me, help me", but nobody could hear. Nobody could hear me. I knew I had to get to the highway. I'm not very good at distances, but I'd say it was 100 yards. And I could see another barbed wire fence ahead and thought, how many more do I have to go through?

'Then I saw two kids on a bike and called out to them to help me. They stopped. They looked at me, they looked at each other, and they looked at me. I must have looked so dreadful. I realise that there are people who don't want to get involved. I understood that. So I called out to them "You don't have to come near me. But please, call the police and call an ambulance. I've been raped and I'm tied and can't move."

'Then an older fellow came and I called out "Look I'm tied, have you got a knife or scissors or something?" And the three of them came over and they just stood there and looked at me. They were so shocked. I saw the shock on their faces. The older fellow, he covered me with an old rag or something. I thought, how thoughtful. It was a touching gesture. He untied me. The three of them carried me over the barbed wire fence and the old man tore his pants as he was carrying me. I remember feeling sorry that he'd hurt himself too. They put me in a truck and the old man said to the boys "One of you come with me as a witness." They put his bike on the truck.

'They took me to a clinic, in Berwick I think, and called the police across the road. But they couldn't touch me. They had to take me to Dandenong. They asked me if I wanted something and I said, I just want to rinse my mouth out. I had a cup of tea and they took me to Dandenong Hospital. I had doctors and police around me. They were all marvellous. I don't know how people can say that police and doctors look at a victim in a dirty way. It's not so. If a person is honest they're on your side and will help you. I told them in detail what happened. I wasn't ashamed. I was just relieved that I was alive.

'The worst part is the emotions. My personal relationships were absolutely horrible afterwards. What happens to a rape victim after is that you have to go on living. When the ordeal is over. The only thing I wanted from the man that I loved was his comfort, encouragement and understanding. He couldn't give that. He thought I'd asked for it. He thought I knew the chap before it happened. He doubted my word.

'That's what hurt me the most. To be doubted. I was working

so hard to try and make ends meet and this thing happens to me. And he doubts my word.

'Emotionally I was crucified by my lover. At one stage I said to him "Between you and the man who raped me, you're the worst. Because you're torturing me mentally and emotionally. He tortured me physically, but you're crucifying me."

'His attitude was so cruel. He'd come to the hospital and bring flowers every day. Twice a day sometimes. But his response to me! He would just sit there or stand there and just look at me like I was some sort of freak. I would say to him "Why don't you put your arm around me? That's all I ask. Just company. Is that too much to ask?" But it was too much to ask, apparently. He couldn't understand. They think you ask for it, that you enjoyed it. It doesn't matter how strong a relationship might be, it's not going to survive. It might survive 12 months or even a couple of years. But sooner or later it'll break.

'That I survived was really a miracle. Since then I've learnt that two skeletons were found. I'm pretty sure those women must have been tied up and left to die. Can you imagine being tied up and left to die? You're still alive — you're dying but you're still alive. Dying from hunger, dying from thirst. That must be the worst kind of death.

'When I think how a person can suffer. Being raped, mutilated and left to die. And there I was lying in hospital getting the best of treatment. With people caring about me, strangers caring about me. I thought to myself, I *have* to do something, even if I have to swallow my pride and throw open my personal life to the whole world. I have to make sure that something is done about it.

'When I came out of hospital a girl I knew was murdered in the Commission buildings in Richmond. She was a singer. A Greek singer in a night club. I'd taken photos of her. She was much younger than me, about twenty-five. She was on her way home from work. She got a lift with her boss right to the doorstep. And they found her in the lift, dead. When I think about these things it kills me. I had a nervous breakdown when I heard about that. I thought I had to do something.

'Then the little Vietnamese girl who was thrown down a

shaft, also in Richmond, also in the Commission flats. Three years old. What does she know about life? Poor kid. She died from the rape itself.

'So I'm not going public for my own sake, although I feel I wasn't treated fairly in regards to compensation. I'm speaking for the past victims who are dead. And for the past victims who are alive but haven't got the strength and the guts to tell it all. Who are probably in mental asylums. I'm speaking for the women who are probably being raped and abducted right now, right around the country. And for the future victims. For the young girls who are growing up now. I want to fight for all these people. I have a responsibility.

'I feel we have to re-educate our menfolk as to how to treat a woman. And we, as a nation, should look after one another. There ought to be some sort of national compensation scheme to protect everybody. It's not enough to just put the man in jail.

'People think, the criminal is in jail and can't hurt anybody. But what about the victim? I haven't got the freedom like I used to. I'm a prisoner within myself. I'm not in jail like he is, but I'm a prisoner. When I go out now I always have to be accompanied by somebody. Or I have to come home early to make sure that the lights of the flats are still on. Little things like that, I always have to do. When I walk down the street I'm afraid. Somebody's walking behind me — I turn quickly around.

'We have to do something to protect people financially. I'm paying seven kinds of insurance. I'm paying Third Party, Comprehensive for the car, superannuation, Medibank. And I have insurance against wages when I'm hospitalised and extra insurance for my teeth. The total of the premium is $1,600 each year, yet I'm still not covered on the street. Or in my backyard. They tell me that in New Zealand there's a scheme that covers everybody, all the time, wherever they are. Against road accidents, industrial accidents, crime.

'Why don't we spend more money on victims? Let's face it, all of us put together make one whole. Let's look after one another. Let's love one another. We listen to songs about love thy neighbour, yet where is all this love? I think it's about time we did something.'

So do I, Valerie. And I don't think that receiving $884 for hospital and medical bills, $2,000 for the impairment of your earning capacity and $4,616 for your pain and suffering is enough. So I'm putting $200 into a fund in the belief that *Age* readers will want to join me. Valerie's financial situation is desperate.

It's also time to look closely at that Crimes' Compensation Act. At the time of Valerie's nightmare, the maximum payable was $7,500. It has now been increased to $10,000 which is clearly inadequate for the victims of serious crime. All it does is give new meaning to the expression 'adding insult to injury'.

POSTSCRIPT:
The public response to Valerie's story resulted in donations of $12,319.

A flotilla of floats

Wandered into town the other day to see *Gandhi*, the thinking man's *E.T.*, when we bumped into the Moomba procession. Hadn't seen it for years, this annual cavalcade that shames the Mardi Gras and scoffs at Rio's carnival. As surely as Melbourne's City Square shames the Red, Times and Leicester. Tumultuous crowds up to two-deep lined the porn-cinema end of Swanston Street as perennial favourites Zig and Zag drove by in their iron lungs, closely followed by, of all things, a Hare Krishna dragging a blue figure at least eight metres long representing the Supreme Lord Vishnu at the birth of the universe. Waving his six arms beneath a head dress of nineteen swaying cobras, it had the most profound effect on a couple of awe-struck derros. Emitting cries of terror, they chucked away their carafe of metho and lumbered off in hot pursuit of the Salvation Army.

That was only one of the flotilla of floats that expressed Melbourne's cultural diversity. The parade was led, for example, by our brave volunteer fire persons and was trailed — and tailed — by hundreds of illegal immigrants hidden in the never-ending Chinese dragon.

So I thought readers might be interested if I gave them a run-down on what we saw betwixt and between, so that they could ring Don Dunstan to make their bookings for *next* year.

Victoria's favourite delinquents, the Broady Boys, rolled by wrecking a train carriage kindly provided by VicRail.

We saw a most amusing race riot between Vietnamese and Lebanese migrants, in a cardboard high-rise building.

The crowds cheered wildly as General Motors workers were run over by a convoy of Camiras with mag wheels and air-conditioning.

The Festival of Light tried to strike terror in our hearts by having midgets in papier mâché masks representing the herpes virus running around pretending to infect the populace. The

Reverend Fred Nile had flown down from Sydney especially, and could be seen painting white crosses on the doors of the aforementioned porn cinemas, with joyful cries of 'Unclean! Unclean!'.

Refusing to be intimidated, the madams and mademoiselles from Melbourne's massage parlours danced joyfully in their wake, spraying clouds of talcum powder in the direction of the populace. Suddenly respectable-looking husbands hid their faces in crisp bags for fear of being recognised by Sabrina from the Sultan's Harem or Darlene from Feels on Wheels.

The Brown Bombers were a particularly unpopular entry as, singing 'We run them in, we run them in', they issued tickets to people standing in the No Standing zones or to kids in the vicinity of expired meters.

A popular favourite with the throngs were the Botanic Gardens' Flashers, although it's a pity that the Lady Mayoress passed out when they indecently exposed themselves in front of the VIPs at the Town Hall.

For years the Botulism Award had been won by Victoria's meat pie manufacturers but this time the mantle went to the Taiwanese who shuffled down Swanston Street under a dirty great mushroom cloud.

There was a serious traffic jam at the corner of Swanston and Collins Streets, caused by members of a number of bankrupt football teams shuffling along with bulging suitcases. It turned out that they really weren't in the procession at all, but were heading for Sydney Road where they hoped to hitchhike their way to lonely exile in northern cities. And if I may be permitted a personal observation, the sooner we get rid of all of them the better.

At about this time, a number of ancient Anzacs shuffled into view, heading for the Shrine of Remembrance. It turned out that someone at the RSL had got the dates wrong.

The *Bulletin* float was very popular, with Pierpont being stoned by the less respectable members of the Melbourne Stock Exchange whilst David McNicoll was torn from the float by geriatric groupies.

A dozen of Melbourne's top real estate agents marched resolutely towards the Melbourne *Herald* burning copies of the *Age* to cries of 'Stamp out socialism!'.

Melbourne's gay community contributed an on-going orgy of naked young men in a mobile steam bath, the heated mists cunningly suggested by wisps of fairy floss.

The new Chairman of the Board of Works, Ray Marginson, contributed a float depicting a dried-up reservoir whilst his loyal lieutenants handed out photographs of water to a public that has long since forgotten what it looks like.

And you felt a great collective lump in the metropolitan throat when a hundred flagellant Liberals, mainly MPs rejected at the polls, shuffled past to the tune of 'We're not waiting for the world' performed by Liberal chanteuse Colleen Hewett. (The up-beat arrangement that had so enlivened our election campaign had been rescored by Mike Brady so that the tune was ingeniously interwoven with the resonant down-beat of Handel's 'Death March'.) And the crowds were reduced to stifled sobs at the sight of the crucified Malcolm Fraser who, as we all know, died to save us all.

Cases of mistaken identity

It's the early days of the Australian film renaissance and I've turned up at Cannes with *Don's Party* and a couple of posters. Naive and trusting, I find myself reeling from the voracious maws of a variety of celluloid carnivores. Piranha, hyena, distributor. So much so that I flee the place, praying that it be obliterated in an appropriately cinematic fashion. For example, wiped off the face of the planet by a giant haemorrhoid from outer space.

Not that there aren't amusing moments. I meet director Werner Herzog for the first time. He's hiding from the German police in Cannes, having shot one of the actors in Berlin. (Having long yearned to shoot actors myself, I am lost in admiration.) Then there's the amusing night I go to one of Cannes's lesser restaurants with two Australian filmies, Festival director David Roe and the ethereally beautiful Sylvie Le Clezio. A few moments later we're forced to evacuate, feeling an attack of diarrhoea about to overwhelm us. Whereupon we get stuck in a lift between the third and fourth floors. We spend twenty minutes screaming out for help. Talk about a race against time.

But I prefer to block out *that* painful memory with one of those Cases of Mistaken Identity, the theme for today. On arriving in Cannes, the mecca for celebrity-spotters, I was besieged by autograph hunters. I knew that the French were passionate about their cinema but had no idea that Australia's new wave had already broken on their shore, that the identities of the Australian contingent were known to them. Nonetheless I signed happily away — books, menus and the odd plaster cast — only to provoke puzzled frowns and disappointed mutterings. Then the centime dropped — they thought I was Peter Ustinov. Paddy McGuinness, then film critic for the *Financial Review*, was also in town causing exactly the same confusion.

A few years later, I was working with Peter Ustinov in

Australia, recording the soundtrack for *Grendel Grendel Grendel*, for which he provided the voice of the melancholy monster. At the end of a recording session, we piled into the hire care and dropped him off at the Boulevard Hotel.

'I've got one of his records', the chauffeur said, as Ustinov barrelled into the foyer. 'One of his records?' I replied, somewhat puzzled. Had Peter done a Spoken Voice album on Pushkin? Had he recorded his memoirs?

'Yeah, the Blue Tail Fly.'

I was, needless to say, astonished. We'd been in the same car for *days* and Ustinov had lived up to his reputation as a raconteur, telling anecdotes of his experiences as a playwright and thespian, and the driver thought he was Burl bloody Ives!

Next day I had to decide whether or not to tell Ustinov the story. Those who've read his autobiography *Dear Me* will have been intrigued by its rather self-pitying tone of voice. Despite his successes as a playwright, actor and film director (his adaptation of Melville's *Billy Budd* was, I think, remarkable), Peter obviously sees himself as having failed. So would the driver's confusion cut him to the quick?

Finally I decided to tell him for the simple reason that I, too, had been mistaken for Burl Ives. A few weeks earlier I'd been at Safeway loading up the trolley when a matron saw me across a crowded freezer chest and insisted that I was the burly American folk singer. I have a distinct memory of being first trailed, then chased by this determined matriarch, her trolley striking sparks as it ricocheted off the trolleys of innocent bystanders. I think she wanted me to autograph her No. 14 frozen Steggels.

So I told Peter the story about the chauffeur and he rolled his eyes to heaven. 'I've been in films for over forty years. I was Nero in *Quo Vadis* in 1951 and won an Oscar for *Spartacus* in 1960. I've been in *The Way Ahead*, *Private Angelo*, *Beau Brummel*, *The Sundowners* and others I've completely forgotten. Yet after you dropped me off yesterday I went for a walk up to the Cross, passing through the crowd as though invisible. Then suddenly I was bailed up by a couple of housewives who said "We know who *you* are!" And, frankly, I was somewhat relieved. But as the conversation continued it became quite clear that they had no idea of my name. "But we saw you on the Mike Walsh Show!"'

Once upon a time film stars dominated the landscape. Now *real* fame belongs to guests on TV talk shows.

(The ephemeral nature of fame recalls a true story from the recent election campaign. Tamie Fraser was visiting a nursing home and the matron told an old lady that the Prime Minister's wife was here to see her. Whereupon the dear old soul looked up, smiled and said 'Hello Mrs Menzies'.)

Which brings me to my latest case of mistaken identity. Now that we fire-breathing radicals are in power in Victoria (as well as almost everywhere else) it's a case of jobs for the boys. So I've been appointed Chairman of the Victorian Council for the Arts, which means I get invited to all sorts of things and places. Having topped the *Herald*'s ten worst dressed men list, just ahead of Normie Gallagher, nobody really *likes* inviting me. Quite apart from my clothes, there's the vexed question of my table manners. But such invitations are a matter of protocol. Which is why I was invited to have lunch, and then go to the opera, with a very famous visiting celebrity. An entertainer who'd become a Minister for Culture. Somebody whose name was a household word.

When we met I couldn't help noticing she didn't look like her colour photos on the record albums. Concluding she only wore glasses when singing, I'd told her how I'd collected *all* her hits and particularly loved the way she sang 'The Three Bells'.

I also asked her if there's any truth in the rumour that she was romantically involved with Frank Hardy.

Frankly, I can't understand why everybody got so upset. Why the whole thing blew into a diplomatic incident. I mean, how was I to know it was Melina Mercouri and not Nana Mouskouri? Anyway, it could have been a lot worse. As I said to the ambassador at the time, 'Well, at least they're both Italians'.

Let downcasts become outcasts

Just returned from India where I did a top secret, hush-hush, mum's the word job for the PM. My task? To study the relevance of Untouchability to the Australian social system to see if our downcasts could become outcasts on a more or less permanent basis.

It's not generally recognised in the west that Untouchability was a marketing coup conceived by the swastika-brandishing Aryans when they invaded the Indian subcontinent somewhere in the year Dot. You see, when they arrived they found the country occupied by a vast number of aborigines who seemed ideally suited for doing all the worst jobs, like sweeping, heavy labouring and cleaning out the loos. But how best perpetually to enslave these Dravidian darkies?

Well, your old Hindus weren't exactly thick. They came up with the idea of *caste*. Though later dressed up in all sorts of religious mumbo-jumbo, the word caste dramatises its real meaning: 'Varda' meaning colour. (Thousands of years later, there's still a tendency for India's Untouchables to be at the under-exposed end of the photographic scale.) But if you think that Untouchables belong to a caste, you're wrong. Just as they're beneath contempt, they're *beneath* caste.

In brief, here's how the caste system worked when Gandhi, the Billy McMahon of Indian politics arrived on the scene. The Vedic, or Old Testament, had castes beginning with Brahma, the creator. So Brahmins, those of the top drawer, sprang from his mouth. The Kshatriyas, soldiers and such like, from his muscles. Vaisyas, the business people, sprang from his thighs, while the Sudras, artisans and craftsmen, came from his feet. The Untouchables? From the dirt beneath. Worse still, the five original divisions had multiplied into 5,000 sub-castes, 1,886 for your hoity-toity Brahmins alone. As Dominique Lapierre comments: 'Every occupation had its caste, splitting society up into a myriad of closed guilds into which a man was condemned by his birth to work, live, marry and die. So precise were the definitions that an iron smelter was in a different caste than an ironsmith.' But an Untouchable was in *none* of them.

The people that Gandhi called Harijans (or children of god) were known as Invisibles in parts of India where they were simply forbidden to leave their shacks during the daylight hours.

Constituting a sixth of India's population, Untouchables were told that their obliterated status was a direct result of alleged sins in past incarnations. If they wanted to be promoted to even the lowest caste, if they aspired to the dregs, they had to behave themselves and do their master's bidding. And remember, *everybody* was an Untouchable's master.

What a neat, elegant idea. You have a permanent sub-proletariat whose role is ordained *not* by social injustice but by cosmic justice. No wonder the Prime Minister is anxiously awaiting my confidential report.

As Dominique Lapierre explains: 'Readily identifiable by the darkness of their skin, their cringing submissiveness and their ragged dress ... their name expressed the contamination that stained a caste Hindu at the slightest contact ... a stain that had to be removed by a ritual, purifying bath. Even their footprints in the soil could defile some Brahmin neighbourhoods. An Untouchable was obliged to shrink from the path of an on-coming caste Hindu lest his shadow fall across his route and soil him ... No Hindu could eat in the presence of an Untouchable, drink water from a well by his hands, use utensils that had been soiled by his touch. Many Hindu temples were closed to them. Their children were not accepted in schools. Even in death they remained pariahs. Untouchables were not allowed to use the common cremation grounds. Invariably too poor to buy logs for their own funeral pyres, their dead were usually consumed by vultures rather than by flames.'

At the time of partition, Untouchables were still serfs in parts of the subcontinent, bought, sold and valued like an ox. They enjoyed only one privilege — their exemption from Hinduism's vegetarian code. 'Whenever an epidemic struck down a sacred cow, the Untouchable who carted off the rotting carcass was allowed to sell the meat to his fellow outcasts.'

To some extent, Gandhi's assassination was provoked by his affection for the Harijans. On arriving from South Africa he'd outraged Hindu opinion by publicly cleaning out an Untouchable's loo. And in 1922 he'd almost died for them in a fast to prevent a political reform that would have institutionalised their separateness from Indian society.

Although the term is now outlawed, Untouchability is still alive and well. Throughout the country I saw people sweeping, endlessly and arbitrarily, almost any piece of open ground. They'd sweep a little pile here, and then sweep a little pile there, in a procedure that was more ritualistic than meaningful. Occasionally a sacred cow would come along and munch at the collection (your sacred cow is a great recycler of everything from scrap paper to plastic bags). And they do the sweeping from a squatting position, as the broom has no handle. Oh, I saw *one* long-handled broom outside the Ashoka Hotel in Delhi, but in the rest of the country this uplifting invention is a closely guarded secret.

Hindu friends also expressed annoyance at the way Gandhi had succeeded in having many seats in the Indian Parliament reserved for the Untouchables, 'whilst they can compete for the rest'. Hence the Untouchables are seen as becoming social climbers and, moreover, climbers with political clout. On the other hand, more seasoned political observers told me that once Untouchables had made it to the upper ranks, they tended to be 'duchessed' by the system and soon lost interest in their lowly electorate. A similar phenomenon has, of course, been observed over the years in the Labor movement.

During the communal slaughter that both preceded and followed partition, the caste system meant that piles of bodies were left besmirching the Canberra-like vistas of Delhi and on more than one occasion, the last vicereine, the admirable Lady Mountbatten, was forced to heave an Untouchable's body onto a truck herself. And in the refugee camps countless thousands of Hindus died rather than take the first step towards preventing plague. Refusing to clean out their toilets, they would demand that the authorities provide them with the necessary equipment, that is, some Untouchables.

Now, I don't think that we'd be able to sell Australia's sub-proletariat the idea of toilet-cleaning too easily. But given the widespread interest in eastern mysticism, we *should* be able to persuade our unemployed that they are, in fact, the children of god. That in some curious way their low status was predestined. Perhaps their parents had voted Labor in a previous incarnation, in which case a few decades of loyal, uncomplaining servitude might, just might, elevate them to the lowest rung of Australia's social ladder in carnations to come. Perhaps in one or two hundred years they might become part-time workers or be permitted the dole.

Just as the Christian church's great breakthrough was to recognise that the best social control was *internal* rather than external — hence the invention of guilt — Hinduism's contribution is to make the down-trodden feel personally responsible for their plight. Instead of complaining about the degradation of their existence, Australia's outcasts, Untouchables, Invisibles, will become submissive and apologetic.

Unfortunately, not many of our Untouchables will be black, so they'll have to be identified by another means. How about an outcast mark between the eyebrows?

This wouldn't be the first time an ancient Hindu idea was recycled for modern use. Look at the way Hitler borrowed the swastika for *his* Aryans.

Magnificent maharajahs

One of the reasons that Australia's GNP is rather RIP is, clearly, because our class system is ill-defined. Your filthy rich are too inhibited to dramatise fully the failure of the rank and file. If you take away their Rolls Royces, yachts and race horses what have you got? Just a few more boring Australians.

Which is why I went to India to research the lifestyles of the maharajahs, in the hope that I could persuade our middle-class tycoons to be more imaginative, more magnificent. In this way the toiling and untoiling masses, respectively, will have something to admire and dream about.

It's a matter of considerable regret that the followers of

Mahatma Gandhi, India's Billy McMahon, had the maharajahs removed from office after Independence. However, while exploring the sub-continent I managed to make contact with a few redundant royals who expressed their willingness to come to Australia to show our filthy rich how to be far filthier.

Which reminds me that the British Secret Service had the most *wonderful* files on the secret and not so secret sex lives of the maharajahs which they burnt before handing Nehru the ignition keys to the ship of state. As might be expected, Nehru violently objected to this lurid bonfire, saying that the files were an important part of Indian history. There can be no suggestion that Nehru would have used the files as effectively as J. Edgar Hoover who, as you know, recorded the peccadilloes of American politicians up to and including the presidents.

The sex lives of our local potentates are distinctly unimaginative, composed of ordinary adulteries and common-or-garden perversions. Whereas your average maharajah was into things that would produce gasps of disbelief (and admiration) from your King's Cross pornographer.

Had Sir Conrad Corfield *not* ordered the historic blaze (he lit it himself) Nehru would have read of a Nawab who had a bet with a number of neighbouring princes to see who could deflower the most virgins in a year. Of the Maharajah of Kashmir who was caught with his jodhpurs down in London's Savoy Hotel by a blackmailer. Of the Nizam of Hyderabad's collection of porn (the old bloke used to record the erotic activities of his guests through peepholes in the bedrooms and bathrooms). Of the unpleasant business of the Maharajah of Alwar who believed himself a reincarnation of the god Rama and, to prevent the contamination of merely human flesh, wore black gloves. Indeed, he refused to take them off to shake the hand of the King of England.

Another interesting part of his ensemble was his turban which his milliner made after Hindu theologians had calculated the *exact* size of the one worn by god. Black gloves notwithstanding, he did permit other fleshy encounters, particularly in the royal bed where aspirants to officer class in his army had to prove their valour. Orgies were frequent, murders were common.

Now meet the Maharajahs of Bharatpur who were so loaded that most of their wealth had to be permanently stored in a cave in Rajasthan. Each incumbent was allowed to visit the treasure just once in his lifetime to select a few baubles for his personal use. Among the goodies was a diamond breast plate (made up of over a thousand princely gems) which he wore once a year under interesting circumstances. That is, apart from the breast plate, he was starkers, so that he could display his splendid erection to the admiring populace. This was all mixed up with religion and Lord Shiva, the engorged member allegedly radiating magic powers.

The Maharajah of Mysore also mixed diamonds with potency, believing that the jewel, in crushed form, was the most potent of aphrodisiacs. As Dominique Lapierre writes: 'That unfortunate discovery led to the rapid impoverishment of the state treasury as hundreds of precious stones were ground to dust in the princely mills. The dancing girls for whom the resulting potions were meant, in a sense, to benefit, were paraded through his state on elephants whose trunks were studded with rubies and whose ears were decorated with elephantine earrings composed of the prince's surviving baubles.'

A Maharajah of Gwalior was determined to outdo Buck. Palace, and so ordered the largest chandelier in creation from Venice. Then doubts were expressed about the strength of the palace roof, so he had his heaviest elephant placed on the roof by a special crane. When the pachyderm failed to crash through the plaster, the aforementioned light fitting was fitted.

The Nizam of Hyderabad had the largest car collection in the country by a simple ruse. Whenever he noticed an amusing vehicle tootling around his landscape, he would advise the unhappy owner that 'his exalted highness would be pleased to receive it as a gift' so by Independence he had literally hundreds of Rolls, Bentleys and what-have-you lying rusting in his garage.

Rolls Royces were particularly favoured by your maharajahs.

The Maharajah of Patiala had twenty-seven of them, and the Maharajah of Bharatpur took the Prince of Wales and Lord Louis Mountbatten out in a Rolls Royce shooting brake. The car, Mountbatten noted in his diary, 'went over wild, open country smashing through holes and over boulders, heaving and rocking like a boat at sea'.

The same chap owned a Rolls that, according to legend, had 'mysterious, sexually stimulating waves emanating from its silver frame' but even this was eclipsed by the Maharajah of Alwar's Lancaster which was gold-plated inside and out. The chauffeur, sitting on a gold brocade cushion turned a sculptured ivory wheel whilst behind him the Maharajah sat in a perfectly reproduced replica of the Coronation Coach of the British royals. It did 70 miles per hour.

The Maharajah of Gwalior was mad on electric trains. His was made up of 250 ft of solid silver rails which ran around a giant dining table. The Maharajah sat at a control panel that enabled him to deliver the various dishes direct from the kitchen, stopping neatly in front of each guest. If you wanted some beetroot or second helpings of pud, the Maharajah would simply pull the appropriate lever. He also enjoyed playing tricks on people, such as having your pancakes decline to stop at your station.

In *Freedom at Midnight* Lapierre describes a memorable banquet in honour of the Viceroy. 'The prince's control panel short-circuited. While their excellencies looked on aghast, his electric trains ran amok, racing from one end of the banquet hall to the other, indifferently sloshing gravy, roast beef and a puree of peas on the Maharajah's guests. It was catastrophe without parallel in the annals of railroading.'

Then there was the Nawab of Junagadh who preferred dogs to people. His lived in sumptuous palaces equipped with 'telephones, electricity and domestic servants' and were buried in marble mausoleums to the strains of Chopin's 'Funeral March'. While the Viceroy turned down his invitation, 150,000 people attended the wedding of his favourite bitch, Roshana, to a labrador named Bobby. Contemporary accounts make the wedding of Charles and Di seem like a quickie at the Registry

Office and an estimate of the budget suggests that the 'do' could have sustained the lives of a good 12,000 unhappy humans outside his palace walls.

The throne of the Nawab of Rampur sat in the middle of a hall, the white marble columns of which were fashioned in the shape of nude women. As *Freedom at Midnight* explains: 'Cut into the rich gold brocade of its cushion was a hole providing direct access to a chamber pot. With an appropriately princely rumble, the ruler was thus able to relieve his royal person without interrupting the flow of the affairs of state.'

While your maharajahs were into harems, the Sikh Sir Bhupinder Singh, the Magnificent, the seventh Maharajah of Patiala, was the daddy of them all. Six ft 4 ins and 300 lbs, his extended family included 350 girls with whom he had congress by means of a wide silk hammock. By raising and lowering himself according to whim, the most demanding positions of the kama sutra were achievable.

To keep his girls up to date, Sir Bhupinder kept a large staff of perfumers, jewellers, hairdressers, beauticians and dressmakers. Plus a team of French, British and Indian plastic surgeons who could alter the appearance of his favourites 'according to the Maharajah's fluctuating tastes or the dictates of the London fashion magazines'.

Enough is enough. I'm sure I've tantalised Australia's ancien and nouveau rich enough. Let us hope that you respond accordingly and *really* give Bubbles Fisher something to talk about.

STOP PRESS: But I had almost forgotten the Nizam of Hyderabad or to give him his full title, Rustum-i-Dauran, Arustu-i-Zeman, Wal Mamalik, Asif Jah, Nawab Mir Osman, Alikhar Bahadur, Musafrul Mulk Nizam al-Mulk, Sipah Solar, Fetah Jang, His Exalted Highness, Most Faithful Ally of the British Crown, the seventh Nizam of Hyderabad. A feeble little chap of 5ft 3ins with betel-rotted teeth, he was forever fearful of being poisoned. So his hapless food taster was forever sampling his unchanging diet of cream, sweets, fruits, betel nuts and a nightly bowl of opium. Regarded as the richest man on earth, he dressed in rumpled cotton pyjamas and sloppy slippers from the local market place. He wore the same dandruff-encrusted fez for over thirty years and, although possessing a solid gold service for a hundred, ate off a tin plate while squatting on his bedroom floor.

While rats ate the millions and millions of dollars in bank notes stuffed in every nook and cranny of his palace, he made Scrooge McDuck look like a public benefactor. Trucks loaded with gold bars were bogged to the axles in his gardens and his diamonds, sapphires, emeralds, rubies and pearls were simply shovelled into cellars.

A visiting doctor, attempting to take his electrocardiogram, found his machine wouldn't work properly. But then, no electrical appliance did — the Nizam kept the palace on half-power.

But my favourite story about the Nizam concerns an annual custom, whereby a ruler's subjects would present him with a gold coin. The procedure was that the ruler would touch it and return it to them. Not so in Hyderabad. The Nizam would grab each piece and plop it in a paper bag beside his throne. On one occasion the gold piece fell, and the Nizam was seen on his hands and knees 'racing its owner along the floor'.

Island of a million burial mounds

The term 'flying visit' has a special relevance to Bahrain, a name at once familiar and mysterious to a million transit passengers. A sort of oasis for Boeings, where the airlines of the earth refuel while their passengers go into a duty-free frenzy. Perfumes, alcohol, cameras, all currencies accepted.

Twenty years ago, the terminal was a ramshackle affair reminiscent of Darwin's. A couple of sheds, a blistered palm tree and a few guards standing around with machine guns. (Barry Humphries and I once gave them an impromptu performance of Hava Nagela to while the time away.) Later, in airline language, they upgraded the facility with the familiar roll-call of duty-free names ... Sony, Pentax, Cartier, Dunhill, Seiko, Veuve Cliquot and Johnny Walker. And in this new terminal there was an archaeological display claiming that Bahrain was the site of the Garden of Eden.

Well, having made fifty trips to the place without ever leaving the airport, I decided to investigate, checking into the anonymous but splendidly efficient Gulf Hotel. Over a breakfast of a Harrod's kipper and some Donald Duck-brand orange juice I read the little tourist guide with growing excitement.

'The Independent State of Bahrain, situated in the Arabian Gulf, has been inhabited by mankind for more than 50 centuries. The word Bahrain literally means "Two Seas" and is a reference to the natural springs of fresh water to be found on the island. Rich in vegetation, the area was once known as the "Island of a million palm trees".'

Looking out of the window, few of the million had survived. One or two punctuated the desert landscape like exclamation marks, but the rest had been bulldozed by building contractors intent on erecting hotels and shopping complexes. Nonetheless, I was convinced that a thorough investigation of the thirty-three islands of the archipelago would be wildly rewarding, given its Old Testament status and its constant mentions in the Babylonian and Sumerian records.

The original Eden ... a strategic port for 5,000 years ... invaded by the Assyrians ... explored by Alexander ... overwhelmed by Islam ... ruled by Persia ... governed by the caliphs of Damascus, Baghdad and the conquering Omanis ... held by the Portuguese in the 15th century to protect their trading routes and haggled over by the Dutch, French and English. And finally seized by the Alkhalifa brothers in the 18th century, the family still in control. With so much history in such a tiny place, where to begin?

Hiring a car and chauffeur, I set out in search of ancient goodies. 'Take me to the enigmatic and world-famous burial mounds, numbering 100,000 and dating back to 2,000 BC', I said, reading from the guide book, 'comprising what is believed to be the world's largest prehistoric cemetery'. So he did. And, sure enough, there were countless identical mounds scattered around most of the landscape. Goose-bumping every vista. The trouble is, after you've seen the first 50 or 60,000 of these funerary mumps, you've seen them all.

So I returned to the guide book and pointed to the bit that said: 'Because of its abundance of water and rich vegetation, Bahrain has long been home to a variety of animals. Camels, horses, the mongoose, the gazelle and various species of lizard.' Nodding vigorously, the driver set off at another tangent across the desert, and an hour later had managed to drum up a single donkey. However he did find another 10,000 identical burial mounds.

Undismayed, I turned to the next page which referred to the feathered population 'date birds, hoopoes, flamingoes, parakeets and a variety of waders'. 'Take me to the wildlife sanctuary in the Zallaqu area', I commanded, stabbing the map with my finger. Whereupon he revved the motor and did a U-turn, taking me through a forest of those oil-pumping machines which reminded me of the Perpetual Motion birds of my childhood, those funny glass toys that kept dipping their beaks into glasses of water. As it happened, the locals had noticed their bird-like qualities and painted the giant machines accordingly, giving them big eyes and yellow beaks. These were the only birds we were to see on our journey, dipping endlessly in the oil fields. No date birds, hoopoes, flamingoes, parakeets. Not so much as a sparrow. However we did see another 30,000 of those fascinating burial mounds.

'The centuries-old craft of pottery making and basket weaving are still practised on the island', I read aloud from the official handbook, but a thorough circumnavigation of Bahrain failed to provide any evidence. There was one giddying moment when I saw a sign saying 'Archaeological Site' which turned out to be half a dozen broken, anonymous slabs of stone all but buried in Coke and Donald Duck orange juice cans. But this trip wasn't entirely wasted as, just nearby, there were another 15,000 burial mounds.

No palm trees, no animals, no birds, no interesting ruins, no centuries-old craft. All but conceding defeat, I begged the driver to take me to the 'extensive museum situated close to the airport containing a multitude of artefacts, some dating back to 2,500 BC, which trace the history of the island and its various inhabitants'. Although engaged full-time in the ferrying of tourists, the driver had never heard of this remarkable establishment so I had to navigate. 'Turn right at the 400th oil rig and then left at the 80,000th burial mound', I said.

Sensing my growing frustration, he decided to excite me by listing the world-famous stars who had, in the last twelve months, performed at the local Bahrain hotels. 'Tony Bennett, Jack Jones, Jose Feliciano, Roberta Flack, and the Stylistics.'

It took us the best part of another hour to find the fabled

museum which turned out to be stuck at the back of some hangars, in the middle of a complex of tin sheds, just to the right of the Blind Institute. It was, needless to say, as firmly closed as your typical burial mound. Subsequent investigations suggested that it was hardly ever open.

By now I felt like going back to the hotel and calling room service or perhaps crawling into one of the burial mounds and calling tomb service. But the driver inflamed my senses by offering to take me to the Virgins' Pool. Needless to say there were no virgins and not much sign of a pool. It looked rather like the Kew Municipal Baths with the plug out.

Back at the hotel, I turned on the telly to see H. H. Sheikh Isa Bin Sulman Alkhalifa, the Amir of the State of Bahrain, meeting a lot of other Sheikhs who'd arrived for a meeting about how to spend their oil billions. Diminutive in stature (I was reminded of Jose Ferrer's performance of Toulouse Lautrec), he had a lot of dignity. As William McMahon and Napoleon Bonaparte remind us, you don't measure stature in inches and, in any case, Bahrain is a very small country.

But while its tourist facilities are disappointing and it fails to live up to the promise of Eden, the state of Bahrain has one thing going for it. The Sheikh insists that everybody involved in government has their number in the phone book. The palace is 661451, you can get the Crown Prince on 661681, the Prime Minister awaits your call on 253361 and 247240 gets you the Governor of the Bahrain Monetary Agency. Then comes a list of the Ministers' numbers — and not just their offices. For example, if you want to call the Minister for Commerce and Agriculture at his residence, it's 713296. And if you want to interrupt the Minister of State for Cabinet Affairs while he's watching *Kojak*, you call 714565.

This splendid expression of open government, so sadly lacking in Australia, enabled me to dial the residence of the Minister for Tourism to tell him what I thought of his museum, his Virgins' Pool, his flora, fauna, burial mounds and 'other places of interest'. But when I rang the residence, there was nobody home.

Dialogue for the unsuspecting traveller

The people who compile phrase books for tourists are either (a) surrealists, (b) sadists or (c) sex maniacs. Let us deal with (a) first, the tendency to foist Salvador Daliesque dialogues on the unsuspecting traveller.

You may remember the Monty Python sketch wherein John Cleese, playing a confused Hungarian, was heard to comment 'My hovercraft is full of eels'. Well, in my experience of phrase books, that's a comparatively *useful* statement. I refer you to the *Teach Yourself Russian Phrase Book* by J. Burnap, MA (Oxon) currently being proffered by leading bookshops. Opening at random, the first conversational gambit Burnap suggests is . . .

'Where is Ulanova's dressing room?'

Where is Ulanova's dressing room? In an old ladies' home at Omsk, that's where. The poor old love's been retired for twenty years. It'd be like having an Australian phrase book with 'I've got the hots for Gladys Moncrieff'. Indeed, if you wandered around the Bolshoi saying 'Where is Ulanova's dressing room?', they'd *know* that it was a password and that you were working for ASIO.

The next suggested exchange is equally dangerous, clearly identifying one as a mole or double-agent.

'What make is this bicycle?'
'I am fond of cycling.'
'Are your brakes in order?'
'Yes, but the chain is a bit loose.'

Anyone who's read his John Le Carré recognises that sort of stuff. It's the way all those homosexual spies from MI5 chat

each other up. Come to think of it, most of them were MAs (Oxon) like Mr Burnap.

Clearly Burnap is *determined* to get all his readers into Lubianka. Consider the following exchange, which I've lifted verbatim.

> 'Who is that speaking?'
> 'This is X speaking.'
> 'Speak more clearly.'
> 'Can I speak to X?'
> 'Ask X to come to the phone.'
> 'Tell him that K rang.'
> 'Hello! We were cut off.'

I'm not surprised you were cut off, Mr Burnap. Anyone ringing up identifying themselves as X and asking to speak to K would find the door of his hotel room kicked in quick smart. And they wouldn't be taking him off to Ulanova's dressing room.

Mind you, Mr Burnap, MA (Oxon) may never have *been* to the Soviet. At the very least, his tone of voice suggests that the bad news of the Revolution has yet to reach him. His dialogues seem to belong to the era of the *Titanic* or *Murder on the Orient Express*.

More verbatim dialogue ...

> 'May I take this chair?'
> 'May I look at the engine room?'
> 'Send me the stewardess.'
> 'Can you bring me some tea to the cabin?'
> 'I feel seasick.'
> 'Can you stand the rolling?'
> 'The sea is very rough.'
> 'Visibility is bad.'
> 'The fog horn is sounding.'
> 'Ring twice for the chambermaid.'

Mr Burnap introduces his volume with a wry donnish smile: 'To the casual reader of any phrase book it must appear that the grim fates pursue the traveller with inevitable disaster. His passport needs renewal, he misses his train, his number is taken by a traffic policeman, he is removed to hospital for observation. The flippant author is, of course, tempted to complete his sections with suitable doom. For example, in mountaineering "The rope is breaking" and again in shopping "I have two right shoes".

'This, however, is no place for flippancy and the author has, he hopes, sternly resisted temptation. Any resemblances to humour are, therefore, entirely fortuitous.'

Well, I don't believe you Mr Burnap. Not when you provide the would-be cinemagoer with such phrases as 'The close-ups were very good', and 'Several of the slow motion shots were funny'.

Indeed, in the entire phrase book there are only two sentences that have the ring of truth and bitter experience. 'Be so kind as to clean the bath' and 'Get me another towel and some soap' are the plaintive cries heard (but not answered) from unfortunates booked by Intourist into the Hotel Russia.

Finally Burnap loses all credibility by suggesting the following exchange . . .

'What roasts have you?'
'Whatever you wish: pork, roast beef, lamb, veal.'

Anyone who's starved to death in a Deluxe Class Russian hostelry will find that more laughable than eels in a hovercraft. And I recall a joke told me, in Moscow, by a dissident friend.

It's before dawn on Gorky Prospekt and a rumour is spreading like wildfire through the snow-bound streets. There may be some meat at the butcher's! As the sun rises, a long queue of people has formed. They stamp and slap at themselves to keep warm. Promptly at nine the door of the butcher's opens and a stern voice says 'Any Jews, leave the queue!' And a few saddened semites shuffle off.

At noon the door opens again and the voice snarls: 'Anyone who is not a communist, leave the queue!' And those without party cards are banished. In the late afternoon, the door opens for a third time and the voice says 'Anyone who is not an old Bolshevik leave the queue!' So that, finally, only three old chaps who were at the storming of the Winter Palace are left. As night falls, the door opens yet again and the voice snarls 'No meat today!' As the old Bolsheviks move away on frozen feet, one of them is heard to mutter 'Those bloody Jews get the best of everything'.

Anyone planning a trip to Moscow would be well advised to avoid Mr Burnap's dangerous advice and to invest $4.95 in a paperback version of *Gorky Park*.

Now let us explore Italy with Collins, and a phrase book reprinted in 1978. Obedient to tradition, it contains its quota of surrealistic phrases such as

'I can't dance the twist.'
'Where can I buy methylated spirit?'
'Yes, I've brought my racquet and balls.'

But the Collins book is, quite clearly, written by one of those aforementioned sex maniacs. As I turned the pages I was *astonished* by the escalating eroticism of the dialogue. What begins as oblique, in the manner of Harold Pinter, finishes up as disgracefully explicit, as in Harold Robbins.

Cross my heart, the following is taken verbatim from the Collins Phrase Book which clearly should be sealed in plastic and put at the back of the newsagents, alongside the Dutch publications on bondage. All I've done is *slightly* rearrange the order.

'That man is following me everywhere.'
'I am an Englishwoman.'
'I shall call a policeman.'
'Help!'
'Who are you?'
'I don't know you.'
'I don't want to speak to you.'

'Leave me alone.'
'That will do.'
'I will give you nothing.'
'Go away now.'
'It is very annoying.'
'Buzz off!'
'Hop it!'
'How much per hour?'
'How much is it for the day?'
'Is there a hotel where we can stay?'
'I want a room with a double bed.'
'I have no luggage.'
'That's going too far.'
'You have plenty of time.'
'Take your time.'
'We are together.'
'A little more.'
'I feel a draught.'
'Please shut the window.'
'Start!'
'Do not go so fast.'
'A little more . . .'
'Hurry up!'
'I think it wonderful.'
'I enjoy every minute.'
'This is really beautiful.'
'Look down there.'
'It's too much!'
'I've never seen anything nicer.'
'Quickly! Slowly!'
'Forward! Back!'
'On this side! On the other side!'
'That's it! That's right!'
'What a guy!'
'Encore!'
'I am so grateful to you.'
'I have a pain here.' (Frankly, we're not surprised.)
'How much do I owe you?'

'The sheets on the bed are damp.'
'Thank you and goodbye.'

Oh, there are a few phrases to camouflage the author's intentions. Such as 'I think I have food poisoning', and 'Which way is the Sistine Chapel?' But in essence, Collins Italian Phrase Book is a scurrilous document.

We know that travel broadens the mind but is it necessary to encourage such moral elasticity?

A Magical Memory Tour

Because of the heavy mail, columns about the past provoke pitiful pleas from the postie. Hence my decision to embrace nostalgia with a passion, giving Melburnians the chance to wallow in their memories. Even as I write, my staff are scouring the Op Shops for props, and carpenters are putting the finishing touches to my obliterated childhood. No, it won't be at all like Disneyland where the past is a pressure-cooked pastiche. I'm determined to achieve authenticity. Right down to the bicycle-pump flysprays and pre-zipper fly buttons.

Our Magical Memory Tour will begin on the corner of Swanston and Flinders Streets, where you'll catch a 1940s No. 48 tram, paying the conductor a shilling, or deener, for your ticket. No new-fangled decimal currency will be accepted. Sitting in the tram you'll see 'Which twin has the Toni?' and 'We too smoke Turf' ads o'er the windows whilst, to your astonishment, Hillmans, Humbers, bull-nosed Morrises,

Austin 7s, Ford Pilots and Standard Vanguards will tootle by, many driven by men wearing genuine Akubra hats. From time to time, paper boys will clamber on board proffering newspapers in which Dr Evatt attacks Mr Menzies over the Petrov affair and there's some concern about unemployment nudging 50,000.

Keep your eye open for a peppercorn and a pine hedge just after you pass Kew's Harp of Erin Hotel. Yank the leather cord and get off at the next stop. There you'll see an iceman about to lift a dripping block onto the hessian bag on his shoulder, but if you ask him nicely he'll knock a few slivers off with his ice pick for you and the kids to suck. Then follow him inside (having shoved ten bob into the galvo letterbox) and enter the lovingly re-created double-fronted weatherboard. Not very spectacular from the outside, but within as wondrous as Wells's time machine.

Feel the worn Feltex beneath your feet in the hall before stepping onto the genuine lino in the kitchen, the geometric pattern so worn you can see the brown coming through. Forget sliced Wettex — eat genuine toast cut from a bum-shaped loaf with a genuine bread knife. We'll hire you a bent toasting fork for thruppence, otherwise known as a trey. And while you're making toast (with the choice of Mira Plum, Golden Syrup or dripping to put on it after) you can listen to one of the two wirelesses. There's the bakelite Mickey Mantle in the kitchen, or the big bugger in the living room with the little celluloid dial and the woofly speaker behind a piece of torn cloth. Programmes include Crosby Morrison, the Search for the Golden Boomerang with Norman Banks, Bob Dyer and Jack Davey, the Caltex Hour, Sanky's Sacred Songs, the Happy Gang and the Hit Parade. Or if you prefer, there's a crystal set in the bungalow, where you can recapture the joys of the cat's whisker and heavy, pre-war headphones.

The Hit Parade? An eclectic collection including Bing Crosby's 'Galway Bay', Patti Page enquiring about the cost of a canine in the window, Spike Jones playing the 'William Tell Overture', the Weavers singing 'Irene Goodnight' and I-can't-remember-who singing 'Leave the Dishes in the Sink Ma'.

Frankie Laine belts out 'Ghost Riders in the Sky', John Charles Thomas sings 'The Green-eyed Dragon with the Thirteen Tails' and Peter Dawson does 'The Road to Mandalay'.

Vintage ads include a Dawsonian baritone singing 'Come along and have a Peter's ice cream, don't you think it's a jolly good idea', and Bushells's splendid anthem

> In every home
> In every place
> Wherever you may be
> It always will be welcome
> That cup of Bushells Tea.

And who could forget the sound of wind and wolves behind a strangled voice saying 'Only one more mile to the post and Buckley's Canadiol Mixture'?

There's an excellent selection of comedy records on which Arthur Askey comes to press his suit, Cecily Courtnege orders a double dozen double damask danner nipkins (danner nipkins?), and Stanley Holloway tells how the lion et our Albert.

Kids will be taken to visit an authentic lolly shop, where they'll stand on a box and look into a little glass case displaying liquorice straps, sherbet suckers and a variety of lurid gob stoppers. Old fashioned ice creams, including wafers and woodspoon Dixies, will be available, while the grocer next door, surrounded by flour, sugar and stuff in *sacks* and butter in enormous slabs, will give the kids broken bikkies. In cornets made deftly from brown paper.

Just as Disneyland offers a variety of centrifugal delights, we'll have any number of rides. Including standing on the running board of an old Chev, sitting in the dicky seat of a Ford, riding in the back of an uncle's truck and sitting beside Grandpa as he says 'Giddup' to his draught horse. There'll be swings from the peppercorns, yabby-catching in a dam and double-dinking on a 1940 Malvern Star with upright handle bars.

Lunch will be provided from a lump of skewered corn beef with string in it, with mashed potatoes and beetroot. Sweets will be a choice of plum pudding containing authentic pre-decimal coinage, or Milk Arrowroot biscuits swollen with boiling water. And we'll provide an authentic grandfather who'll sit across the table ignoring everyone, reading the newspaper propped up on a White Crow Tomato Sauce bottle.

By now some visitors will be suffering withdrawal symptoms from a lack of TV. For them, compromise in the form of a 17-inch Astor screening murky kinescopes of the 1956 Olympics, Robyn Farquhar and Don Bennetts in the Hit Parade, Sergeant Bilko and Doberman, early Dobie Gillis episodes featuring Maynard G. Krebbs and historic footage of Graham Kennedy ad-libbing Alka Selzer commercials. There'll also be Interludes of yachts on Albert Park, visits to Professor Browne's Study and Eric Pearce introducing Epilogues. Plus Happy Hammond, Princess Panda, We're happy little Vegemites, and Bobby and Dawn.

Kids will be introduced to the wonders of primitive technology, such as the fly-swatter (blowies provided), the chain-pull toilet (with an old telephone book and pieces of torn newspaper hanging from a nail) and the hand-wringer (complete with soggy washing). The more adventurous will be able to empty the green water from beneath the ice chest or the chamber pots from beneath iron beds. They'll be allowed to paint the stove with silver frost, feed the chooks and watch the way the decapitated rooster runs around the woodyard. No expense will be spared on re-creating yesterday in all its splendour and its horror.

Kids will be taught how to pinch golf balls on the adjacent links, play long-forgotten games like marbles and Cowboys and Indians, and make engine noises with their mouths while pushing Dinky cars in sandpits. (So many basic skills have been lost in this era of electronic games that come complete with the colour and the movement, doing everything but play themselves.) And visitors on Saturdays will be able to catch *another* tram to the rebuilt Rialto in Kew, where they'll see Sam Katzman serials, Tom and Jerry cartoons and Johnny Weissmuller in *Tarzan and the Leopard Woman*. Polly Waffles, Violet Crumbles and other authentic fare will be available at interval and they'll be taught to sing the Hoyts Children's Cinema Club anthem

>Here we are again
>Happy as can be
>All good pals
>And members of the CCC.

Afterwards they'll be able to shoot each other with loaded fingers, dying repeatedly on the wet grass at the Holy Trinity Church.

The day will end with community singing around the piano or pianola, or the quiet hour staring into a fire made from mallee roots. An episode of *When a Girl Marries* (for all those who are in love or for those who can remember) will be interrupted for the tragic news from Buckingham Palace that King George VI has passed away.

From time to time we'll be adding new experiences to our re-creation of yesteryear, including an old style library fully stocked with William, Biggles and Billabong books, a 1940s scout hall with an audio animatronic Arkela, a stormwater drain for perilous exploration and an early post-war State School complete with a behind-the-shelter-shed for early sexual experiments. And boys will be able to compete in the lovingly re-created urinal, seeing how high up the wall they can get.

Yes, we're already taking bookings for our old-style Chrissie holidays, offering a choice of guest houses in Healesville and camping trips to the tea-tree at Rosebud.

Any readers having ideas, artefacts or ageing rellos are asked to write. Best prices paid.

One Summer of Happiness

Yes, it was sad about Ingrid Bergman. Yet I felt a greater sense of loss on reading of the death of another, less famous Swedish actress. The star of my first 'foreign' film, the first movie I saw with writing on the bottom, she died within a few days of Bergman, of the same disease, and rated only a tiny para. on page 12. The film was *One Summer of Happiness* and her name was Ulla Jacobsson.

It was the early 1950s and Melbourne, one of the WASP capitals of the world, had yet to emerge from the Ming Dynasty. While the tyrannies of distance, censorship and provincial smugness kept us safe from stimulating ideas, the culture of the reffo and the wog (official euphemism: New Australian) was just beginning to challenge our suburban certainties.

I vividly recall the suppressed excitement of sitting on stools in a new-fangled espresso bar while a vesuvial machine, as streamlined as a Studebaker, dispensed fragrant, frothy 'cappa-chino'. 'Grazias', we said, our pronunciation more Spanish than Italian. Whereupon the romantic, supercilious young man in his white coat answered 'Prego' with just a hint of mockery.

We were learning that spaghetti wasn't necessarily a pasty mess that mums heat in the tin before up-ending on toast, and that wine could make you just as drunk as beer. And we consummated our love affairs with things Italian by riding Vespas in *de rigueur* duffle coats. Not that you really *rode* a Vespa: they were more like motorised suppositories.

Overnight the city was clogged with we two-stroke centaurs pursuing our Vespa situations, with copies of Albert Camus and Samuel Becket in our army-surplus haversacks.

Ivy growing in chianti bottles. The first tentative explorations of alien cheeses. The discovery that loaves of bread didn't have to be shaped like bricks or buttocks (square and high-tin respectively) as bakers, just like poets, could have their fantasies. On the one hand, our pulses quickened to Bill

Haley and the Comets. On the other, we acned intellectuals saw ourselves as *European*.

Before Ulla Jacobsson, cinema had meant fillums. Sam Katzman serials — will Batman and Robin be turned into zombies by the fiendish Japanese in his secret laboratory beneath Coney Island? Johnny Weissmuller thumping his pectorals. The moist musicals of Miss Esther Williams. Bwana Devil in 3-D at the Esquire. Marlon Brando astride a Harley Davidson. But once you traded in your stove-pipe trousers and crêpe shoes on a duffle coat, corduroys and Dylan Thomas, you had to entertain the possibility of going to the Savoy, the cinema that showed arty films in Russell Street.

So, that's how I first saw Ulla. Whereupon fillums became Films and, just as remarkably, nuddy became Nude.

One Summer of Happiness was the talk of the town. Or rather, the well-informed whisper. For here was a love story in which the Scandinavian Romeo and Juliet got their gear off! Went swimming together. Lay on the grass and embraced. Needless to say, it was all perfectly decorous and understated but for the early 1950s this gentle little film represented the most full-frontal of attacks. In the story, the lovers had to contend with the thin-lipped Calvinism of their remote village. And it would be hard to imagine a more thinly lipped Calvinist remote village than Melbourne.

It took a lot of courage to go to the Savoy for the first time. Finally, whether it was all that cappuccino heating the blood or simply the sap of puberty rising, we made it across the foyer. And in ninety enthralling minutes our lives were changed forever. We realised that foreign countries weren't merely travel posters, that human relations could be filmed with a simplicity that would have horrified Hollywood, and that there was something beyond sex — beyond shelter-shed gropings and back-stall fumblings — that involved a deep and transforming emotion.

For me, and some of my friends, *One Summer of Happiness* was like a tertiary education. We went into the Savoy as smutty little boys and came out as lovers. The only impediment to our maturation process being a very serious shortage of girls to love, particularly young ladies capable of understanding the deep, spiritual significance of removing their gear in the long grass around the Studley Park boat sheds.

Thinking back, I believe it was *One Summer of Happiness* that made me determined to become a film maker. Apart from anything else, it proved that movies didn't need to be on an enormous scale, deafeningly orchestrated, as technicoloured as a Darrel Lea window. You could make a film with half a dozen actors in a simple, rural landscape without a solitary set. And you could make it *matter* by involving recognisable emotions of ordinary, or fairly ordinary, people. So when Barry Jones and I finally went round the world to see how we might revive the Australian industry, it was no accident that we made a bee-line for Stockholm. It was the Swedish industry, not America's, that was to be our model.

It's both odd and banal the way we measure our lives in books, films, popular songs — things that have a strange ability to live outside time, in their own time. Ingrid Bergman's *Casablanca* was shot on a back lot in Hollywood and had precious little to do with reality. Yet with every passing year, the authority of that strange little film grows, so that for millions Bergman's *Casablanca* is a far more real and plausible place than the ramshackle city of real life.

And after many seasons of mixed emotions (winters of discontent, autumns of regret, and springs of optimism) there'll always be, for many of us, *One Summer of Happiness*. It was one of perhaps a dozen films that, along with a dozen novels, helped me grow up.

A few years later I met an astonishingly beautiful sixteen-year-old girl who was to become my wife. The first film we saw together was the overwhelmingly romantic Soviet film *The Cranes are Flying*, about the tragic collision of love and war. And the second film, or perhaps the third, was *One Summer* which the Savoy had thoughtfully revived. As a matter of fact, it was probably one of the last films the Savoy showed before the curtains closed for the last time.

We still remember how we felt floating down the stairs, enchanted and saddened by what we'd seen. Holding hands very, very tightly. Twenty years later Bo Wideberg, another Swedish director, would make a similar film called *Elvira Madigan* and a new generation of lovers would be equally grateful.

These days, the screens are full of escalating horrors and ever madder Maxes. The carnage on the screen is as indiscriminate and unimportant as the electronic detonations in a game of Space Invaders. There are all too few life-enhancing, loving films. In the umpteen Australian films I saw for the AFI judging, naked bodies abounded. But they were stripped to be stabbed, hacked and mutilated. In *One Summer of Happiness* skin was to be touched in thoughtful wonderment. With a tenderness that seems very old fashioned.

So I shouldn't be surprised that Ulla Jacobsson has died. A woman in her fifties. But somehow the news made me feel very, very old. I'm used to policemen looking like boys in borrowed uniforms. I'm reconciled to a world where you have to tell your teenage daughters about the Beatles. I can cope with an accelerating chronology that will soon have the war in Vietnam as remote as Agincourt. I don't really mind having outlived the bouffant and the duck's bum haircut, the Humber Super Snipe and the Goggomobile, the 17 ins Astor and the round-shouldered refrigerator. I can live without the 45 rpm record and the flying saucer, the Windsor knot and the indigenous hamburger, the Lockheed Elektra and William Dobell, the Goon Show and Li'l Abner, the Oslo lunch and creamy soda, the Epilogue and Lee Gordon Presents. I've long since reconciled myself to the fact that buildings rise and fall in our cities, like slow-moving pistons, and have observed, over and over again, how the slogans of old political battles flake off the viaduct walls. But I really wasn't ready to read that Ulla Jacobsson had kicked the bucket. Though I haven't seen the film for well over twenty years, I can still see her face, brimming-eyed and beautiful.

The little para. on page 12 made me feel I'd stepped on an abandoned roller skate. Intimations of mortality are all very well, but this was so blunt, so unequivocal. Recognising that grief is largely self-pity, I can't see why Ulla couldn't have lived to a good old age like Mae West and Fred Astaire.

The Rialto's gone, along with the Esquire, the Lyceum and the Majestic. As for the Regent, it's a ruin haunted by the ghost of Victor Mature in *Demetrius and the Gladiators*. The Legend, my first espresso bar, has gone with the wind and they've so completely obliterated the Savoy that I'm not sure exactly where it was any more. No one knows better than I that tempus is very fugit and, frankly, it's good to outlive the Sullivans and out-distance the *Young Doctors* and the *Restless Years*. But is it absolutely necessary to make *One Summer of Happiness* seem as venerable as *Hamlet*?

But don't worry Ulla. In the suspended animation of the cinema, and in my imagination, you're still just twenty-three.

A morceau of Marceau

Last Friday Channel 7 asked me to interview Marcel Marceau for their late-night rock programme, *Night Moves*. As I was booked for an equally surreal encounter (talking to fifty Ministers at the Kew Baptist Church), this was impossible. However I did catch up with M. Marceau a little later, and here is the unedited transcript...

PA: It's a très big privilege to be ici avec you this morning. Indeed, I must say merci for giving us a morceau of your time, Monsieur Marceau.

MM:

PA: Lovely weather.

MM:

PA: I take it from the way you're leaning into an imaginary wind, that you're finding Melbourne a petit gusty? Oui? Well, as the saying goes, it's an ill vent that blows nobody some bon.

And it's très bon that you have, as it were, blown into Melbourne for your first...

MM:

PA: Sorry, *second* temps. Now, perhaps at the outset you could tell us something of the histoire, as it were, of vôtre arts et metiers. I refer, naturellement, to mime. Where did this practice of wordless gesture originaire?

MM:

PA: Fascinating. Absolutement fascinating. I didn't know about the role of mime or pantomime in Greek and Roman theatre. And I take your point that the representation of emotions and actions by bodily movements and gestures has occurred in all primitive cultures, in Maori war dances, in the Aboriginals' animal mimicry and in the sacrificial rites of the Aztecs. And, yes, I'd have to accept your arguments about the stylised artificialities in restoration comedy, the conventionalised symbolic acting of the Chinese opera or the Japanese No drama, and such comedic performances in silent films as Charlie Chaplin's and Buster Keaton's. But can it *really* be suggested, as you have today, that actors who speak their roles are also mimes?

MM:

PA: Monsieur, as you can see I'm attempting to record this interview on my little tape recorder and I'm afraid the batteries are getting un petit flat. So I wonder if you wouldn't mind miming directly into the microphone? And un petit louder? Merci. Now Monsieur, I understand that vous was un mime right from vôtre childhood. That even in your pram, that is your *landau*, you were entirely silent. Instead of crying, you simply summoned your mother with eloquent gestures.

MM:

PA: Fascinating, absolutement fascinating. Let's imagine that you're at the dentist and he's drilling away at one of vôtre dents, he hits the nerve. Would you yield to the temptation to have un yell?

MM:

PA: You'd what him in the whats?

MM:

PA: Oh, in the boules. Well, that should achieve much the same effect. After all, why should vous be the only one to suffer. But there must be times when you really *do* want to scream.

MM:

PA: I see, during stupid interviews. Well, moving right along, what are your first...

MM:

PA: Pardonez moi, *second* impressions of Melbourne?

MM:

PA: Could you elaborate on that....?

MM:

PA: Well, isn't that bloody typical. Some frog lands at Tulla and within cinq minutes he's a bloody expert. If there's one thing that gives me a pain in the derrière it's you celebrities coming ici and mal-mouthing us Melburnians. I bet you haven't even seen the Paris end of Collins Rue? Or been to some of our bon frog cafés. Well, let me tell you un thing or deux. I reckon that

Paris'd be très bon if it wasn't for the Frenchmen. Talk about arrogant! Looking down their nez at we tourists. Cripes, I lost count of the temps I wanted to give your taxi drivers a knuckle sandwich.

MM:

PA: Don't you mime at me like that!

MM:

PA: Don't you raise your gestures at me! I didn't come ici to be insulté par vous!

MM:

PA: What didn't you say to me? How dare you not say a thing like that! If you think I'm going to sit here and not listen to your insults you've got another think coming!

MM:

PA: So I am a bit gros. At least I don't go mincing around in long underpants and ballet shoes. With my visage all covered in paint blanc. With un fleur sticking out of mon chapeau! I told 'em I didn't bloody well want to interview vous anyway. A ratbag who wanders around the stage all nuit en silence! At the prix you're charging for les billets you'd expect a bloody soundtrack! Who do you think you are anyway? Harpo Marx?

MM:

PA: Just you gesture that encore! Just you step à l'extérieur and mime that!

MM: !

PA: How dare you say that about our Prime Minister! Anyway, Mitterand's a poofter!

MM: !!

PA: And Gough Whitlam could beat Napoleon any time!

Anyway, the spire on our Arts Centre's going to make the Eiffel Tower look like a bill spike! And what about your rotten bombe atomique tests dans le Pacific.

MM: (thump)

PA: Ouch! You've given me a blood nez! You better watch it, Marceau. My big frère est un gendarme!

At this point, the interview est fini.

Butts, barrels and bullets

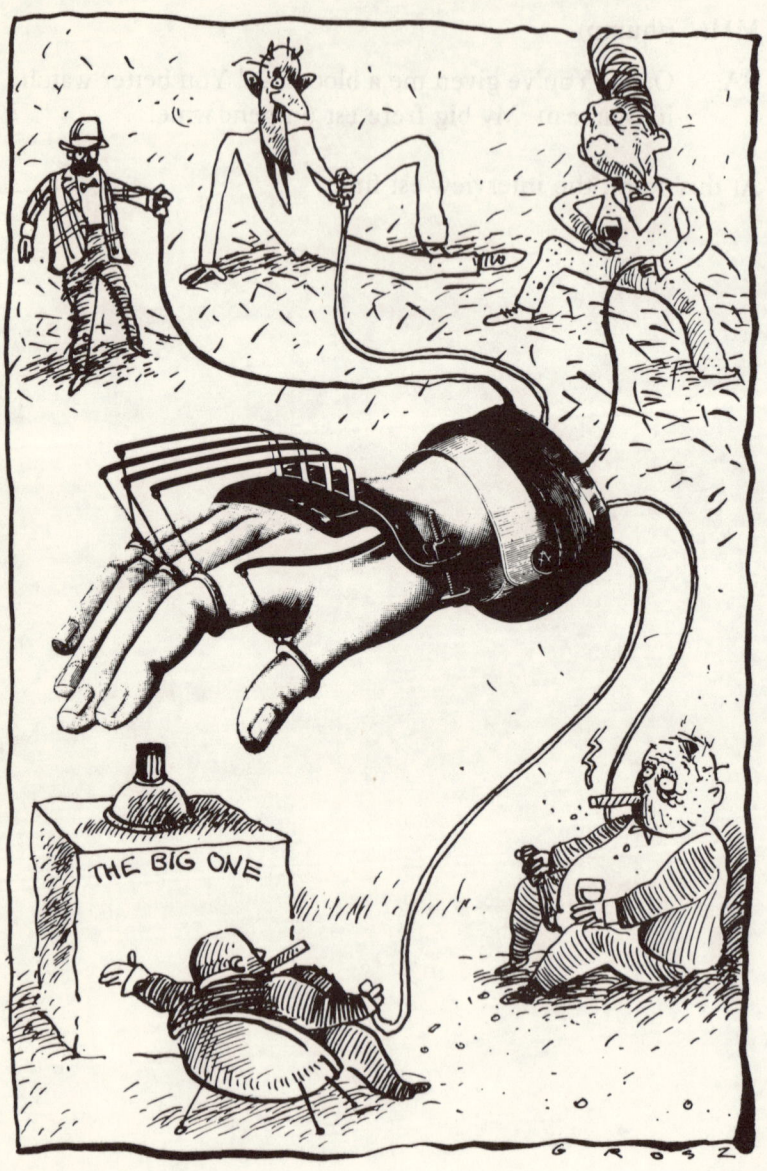

The razor, the hammer, the knife and the gun are not merely objects, or tools, but active verbs. They are provocative. They are demanding. They lure the hand, the fingers. They demand our collaboration. They're a call to action.

Take the cut-throat, so chillingly named. Within its curved, flat flanks is an elegant, murderous blade stropped to sharpness. Fascinating and repelling, it has the hypnotic ability to suggest, to *compel* its own usage. And not merely to scrape off some stubble. You've only to look at a cut-throat to know that it's thirsty for blood, to be reminded of human vulnerability, to realise why Sweeney Todd went into the meat pie business.

Though they're not as sinister, there's something similarly suggestive about scissors. Lying on a table, staring up with their empty metal eyes, they lure the fingers. The blades *want* to be opened, want to slice through paper, cut their swathe through cloth. It requires a conscious effort to hold back, to deny them.

A compass compels us to describe an arc. A dagger wants to glide from its sheath with a whisper. And a gun, particularly a hand gun, wants to fulfil its destiny. The willpower that seems to emanate from these chill little machines results in the death of 15,000 US citizens per annum. Cops perforate robbers and vice versa. Assassins puncture presidents.

Yet the right to bear arms is obsessively defended as, intent on rolling out another million barrels, the gun lobby says 'Guns don't kill people, people do'. It's almost as if guns were morally superior to humans and had inviolate rights under the Constitution. Next thing Detroit will be demanding the vote for Chevrolets, Pontiacs and Dodges.

I remember going into a gun shop in San Francisco, a sort of boutique for butts, barrels and bullets where Magnums and Barettas were displayed as seductively as the finest perfumes. And I *felt* the way one's hand is drawn to a revolver, the way the hand wants to wrap around it (no ifs, no buts) while the finger seeks the curve of the trigger. A gun demands that you point it . . . in the same way that a ballpoint wants you to doodle and a remote control wants you to change channel or adjust the volume.

Not every tool has this power. The drill, the buzzer, the stopwatch — they all attract our attention and intervention, as surely as the telephone dial or Rubik's Cube. But while the keyboards of typewriters, pianos and calculators invite the fingertips and while the hammer seeks the nail, I'm untouched by the entreaties of the motor mower. As far as I'm concerned it can sit in the shed and go rusty. But where the response is simple, uncomplicated and immediate, the human being is almost a tool of the tool. The hapless collaborator. The innocent and sometimes injured party.

All of which brings us to the nuclear bomb. To the ICBM. To the heat-seeking missile. To the skulking submarine. Such weapons, like hammers and scissors, refuse to remain passive. They demand to be freed, to be fired.

How ever human beings want to avoid a nuclear war, how ever hard they might try to negotiate treaties, to be sane and reasonable in their global transactions, the weapons have a mind of their own and there's reason to fear that we'll do their bidding.

Already a whole generation of atomic weapons have become veritable antiques. Geriatric. In many a missile, torpedo and warhead, the chemicals are deteriorating and as fast as new ones roll off the apocalyptic assembly line, others are pulled apart, broken up, scrapped. Well, our nuclear weapons won't take this lying down. They want to rise from their underground silos like the erections of gods. They want to ejaculate doom. And sooner or later, they're going to find a political leader who's so weak willed, so impotent, that he'll fulfil their ambitions.

Imagine, for example, that there was a President who'd been an unsuccessful actor. A sort of B-feature buffoon who never got the girl, let alone the Oscar. Imagine that he's only got a few years left to live and that he realises he can't take it with him. Well, if that's the case, why should anyone else have it? And perhaps he *can* take it with him in another sense. All he has to do is to reach out to touch the red button. It might be an apocryphal red button, but it's there. And in the next decade, more and more dangerous old men will have one.

Whoever wrote the line 'They shall beat the swords into ploughshares' understood the sinister appeal of the weapon, the way it seduces the human sensibilities. But change the weapon into something less glamorous, into something requiring *work*, and you've solved the problem. I may not cease from mortal fight, nor shall the sword sleep in my hand, but I've no urgent desire to go out and plough a paddock. On the basis of personal experience, I think they should beat nuclear weapons into motor mowers. Then we could all sit back and watch the grass grow.

One machine that's proving irresistible is the electric chair. After decades attracting dust and cobwebs, these pop-up toasters for people are popping up again. With more and more destined to die in showers of sparks and blazes of publicity, soon Death Row will be indistinguishable from Broadway.

Mind you, the electric chair doesn't have quite the macabre attraction of the guillotine, introduced to the French National Assembly in 1789 by Dr Joseph Ignace Guillotin. 'My machine will take off a head in a twinkling', he said proudly, 'and the victim will feel nothing but a slight sense of refreshing coolness on the neck. We cannot make too much haste, gentlemen, to allow the nation to enjoy this advantage.'

Not that Dr Guillotin invented the decapitator. It had been shortening the naughty for at least 300 years, under a variety of names. The Scots, for example, called their variant the Maiden.

Dr Joseph first urged the guillotine on democratic grounds. Why should aristocrats have the exclusive privilege of being beheaded? Later the argument became humanitarian — that refreshing coolness.

There's a popular myth that Dr Guillotin became a victim of his gadget. If only justice were that poetic. Though he was imprisoned during the terror, he died peacefully in his four-poster. C'est la mort.

Unidentified flying object

They were loath to wake the President. But it was clearly a matter of national security. So Haig knocked politely on the door of the historic Lincoln bedroom.

The first to stir, Nancy shook Ronnie's shoulder. 'Dear, you'd better put your toupee on.'

So Ronnie reached for his sleek, tonsorial appliance, the wig that had allowed him to say, with honesty, throughout the election campaign, that 'I never dye my hair'. Mind you, the news that Al gave him a few seconds later almost flipped it.

'Mr President . . . I'm afraid you'll have to come to the Ops room. There's something on the radar screens that we simply cannot identify. The computers can't compute it program-wise and the chiefs of staff believe that we're in a confrontation situation that, strategy-wise, may be outside our parameters. Therefore we need your top-level input and . . .'

'What are you trying to tell me, Al?'

'There's a funny blip in the radar and we don't know what to do.'

They descended by lift into the bunker beneath the White House. Protected by 300 ft reinforced concrete, it was where Armageddon would be orchestrated in the event of a commie double-cross or a pre-emptive strike. The President sat in his swivel chair, looking at the great screen that pin-pointed the positions of his bombers, ICBMs, cruise missiles, satellites and submarines — with three red phones in easy reach. The first was labelled Hot Line. The second, Very Hot Line, and the third 'Tony's Pizza. We Home Deliver'.

'This is just the time when the commies would make their move', said the President through clenched dentures. 'Just when Washington's slowing down for Christmas. Just after our Oval Office party when everyone's feeling hung-over. Golly-gee, but those Ruskies are fiends!'

'Yes, Mr President', assented Haig, affirmative-wise. 'That's what comes from negotiating with atheists.'

'And they don't believe in God, either', said the President.

'Mr President', said General Roscoe Sherman III, giving the leader of the free world a very snappy salute, 'let me give you a situational up-date. What we have here may not necessarily involve the Russians.'

'Not the Ruskies', said the President, 'golly gee willikers! You mean the Chinese? But didn't Richard Nixon say they were our buddies?'

'No sir, not the Chinese either. What we may be dealing with here is an ETI!'

'An ETI?' asked the President, searching for a black jellybean in the bowl by his computer console.

'An extra terrestrial intelligence.'

'A UFO', nodded Haig, affirmative-wise.

'Wow!' said the President, who was instantly reminded of the film in which Michael Rennie and a huge silver robot landed in Washington, just near the Monument. From memory, it was a 20th Century Fox production way back in 1951. With Pat Neal before she had her coronary. Directed by Bob Wise.

'Well sir, we're puzzled by certain aspects of the information we're getting. As you can see from the screen, the craft is flying lower and slower than what we'd expect. And it just doesn't line up with any known Soviet technology.'

'Golly gosh! How big is it?'

'We estimate it's about 40 ft long — but it's only moving at about 30 miles per hour. Because it's so low, it got right in under our radar. It's clearly headed here for Washington and is computed to arrive in an hour. A little after midnight.'

'And Mr President, almost the entire White House staff is blind drunk', murmured Haig, confession-wise.

'And they're not much better at the Pentagon. Just when what we're frontally facing is a scenarioisation of conflict in totality.'

'Sir, we've got a flight of jet fighters on the way to intercept now that the craft has penetrated US air space. As you can see, it's just crossing the border into Alaska and we should be hearing from our men at any second.'

'Simmonds!' snapped Haig, 'punch up the radio signals.'

Suddenly a loud crackling noise filled the Ops room. 'Geezus Christ, I don't believe it!' They heard a pilot shout.

'It can't be!' came the voice of a second. This was immediately followed by a terrible explosion and a silence.

'What happened!' gasped the President.

'They collided. Whatever those men saw, it gave them such a surprise that they smashed into each other.'

'Well, what do we *do*?' said the President.

'At this interface between what we know and what we've yet to learn', said Haig, 'it's hard to be specific decision-wise.'

Thoughts whirled through the President's head. What would Henry Fonda do at a time like this?

'Excuse me, sir', said a young officer, saluting to General Sherman III, 'Our electronics boys have just come up with something. The UFO is not from outer space. By computer-enhancement of very faint signals picked up in Pine Gap in Australia and at our early warning station in Alaska, it seems that the craft came right across the North Pole, originating from a base in the Siberian region.'

'So it *is* those damn Ruskies', said the President, pounding his fist on the console so that the jellybeans danced in the bowl.

'Are you going to call Mr Brezhnev on the Very Hot Line?' asked Haig.

'No, goddammit', said the President, with a John Wayne, True Grit-style scowl. 'If those commie bastards think they can get away with a sneak attack, another Pearl Harbor, they've got another think coming.'

Al and General Sherman snapped stiffly to attention as the President gave his orders.

'First of all, shoot down that sneaky missile of theirs. Then, turn the USSR into a parking lot.'

'Affirmative, your presidentiality', said Haig.

In the next few seconds the full might of the US was dramatically demonstrated. A heat-seeking missile zeroed in on the UFO whilst giant ICBMs were launched at Moscow, Leningrad, Omsk and Tomsk. Simultaneously cruise missiles and

Polaris submarines zeroed in on a thousand military targets. It was all over in an hour.

'Well sir, we did it. The USSR is no more', said General Sherman III. 'They must have been over-confident or something. We hardly heard a peep out of them. Oh, they got a few missiles off and wiped out New York and Chicago, but apart from a few out of the way places like Europe and Australia, there's not much damage at all. We estimate that a few hundred million will die in agony because of the giant radioactive cloud that's moving around the planet. But all in all, World War III is over and we've won it.'

'Gee that's swell', said the President, 'Nancy will be thrilled.'

'Mr President', said a young officer, 'a helicopter has just landed by the burnt-out remains of that unidentified Soviet craft. Any second now we'll be able to hear exactly what it was.'

Once again, they heard a pilot's voice crackling through the hi-fidelity speakers around the Ops room. 'Everything is very still as I descend. Very quiet. The Russians' craft came down in a pine forest. Looking down I can see broken branches and a couple of smouldering trunks. I'm moving towards the crash scene now. I see strange, smouldering shapes on the ground. Brightly coloured fragments spread everywhere by the detonation. And there's what's left of the body of the pilot. He's dressed in a strange sort of red costume.'

'Do you hear that Al?' said the President, 'a *red* costume.'

'Oh my God!' came the voice through the speakers. 'Oh my God, what have we done! Oh, this is terrible. Horrible. Ghastly!'

'Get hold of yourself discipline-wise', snarled Haig into the microphone. 'Behave like an American!'

'I'm sorry sir, but this is just *awful*.'

'Young man, haven't you seen death before?' snapped General Sherman III.

'Yes sir. But you don't understand. What we've done is . . . shoot down Santa Claus.'

High-tech. toys

The Arms Race is nothing beside the Toy Race. Escalating in price, complexity and aggression, modern toys employ the same microchips as missile systems and are every bit as menacing. Today's toy boxes are Pandora's boxes full of Pentagonian power-tripping. From Draughts to Space Invaders in three easy decades: childhood has been sucked into a black hole of high tech. and low imagination.

Reeling from the culture shock of Christmas shopping in the 1980s, I found my mind wandering back to the prezzos of the past, to the things that enchanted a child of the 1940s.

In the beginning, there was the toy car, made from pressed tin, propelled by hand with oral sound-effects. Going 'vroom vroom', you crawled around the Feltex, steering your vehicle between the legs of chairs and tables. Or perhaps you had a clockwork car or a broad-gauge Hornby train set. If so, the mechanism would be ruined within hours by over-winding. Only one kid in the neighbourhood was known to have an authentic *electric* train but, of course, his parents were fabulously wealthy. So much so that their dunny was *inside* the house.

My first toy car had a picture of the driver printed on the front windscreen, looking steadily ahead. If you turned the car sideways, his face was printed profile on the side windows. The kid next door had a bus of brightly painted tin, with the faces of passengers (the same passengers) printed down both sides.

Far more desirable were the first Dinky toys, solid little model cars with (rapture!) removable rubber tyres. At the other end of the scale was the metal pedal-car manufactured, as I recall, by Cyclops. Furious knee-pumping could get you up to one or two miles per hour.

Cowboy suits were popular, with Tom Mix-style hats and leather chaps that made you look very bandy. In the westerns, cowboy heroes wore even more elaborate versions, as if their legs were enclosed in giant caterpillars. Then, suddenly, cowboy hats began to shrink and chaps disappeared entirely from the westerns. Modern fashions were imposed, retrospectively, on the wild west.

I can remember falling in love with the first of the post-war cap pistols, a gleaming creation in a toy-shop window in Bridge Road, Richmond. Presented in vivid chromium with plastic pearl handles, it was the most wondrous, bedazzling object. And it fired a coil of caps that left the most satisfyingly acrid scent in the air. Before this, one had been armed with the most pathetic pop-gun which would feebly eject a tethered cork. It was so absurdly de-sexing that you'd prefer to use your fingers, going 'ksssh! ksssh!' with your mouth. But ah, my chromium and plastic cap pistol, that was something. To be quick-drawn from one star-spangled holster and hidden under the pillow at night.

Then there was the Meccano set, those green girders and red metal plates that enabled you to build Heath-Robinson machines and aeroplanes completely devoid of aerodynamics. Once again, the rich kid with the real electric train had the biggest Meccano set you'd ever seen, enough to construct towers, bridges and giant cranes.

He also had a donkey engine that actually putt-putted away burning methylated spirits. He could use it to drive Meccano machines full of pulleys and windmills.

He also had a plastic crystal set with heavy black headphones that enabled you to hear the cricket broadcast being relayed by 3DB from England. Not today's blow-by-blow description of course. Every few minutes they'd announce that somebody had been bowled out or that Bradman had hit a six. I can still remember my wonderment at the way touching a piece of coiled wire to a rough chip of mineral could produce voices and music from the air.

Many of the best toys were purloined from the Kew tip — broken wirelesses, battery cases and mysterious pieces of machinery. Instead of doing everything for you like the modern toy, you had to give them meaning and function by an exercise of imagination. For all its cleverness the modern, high-tech. toy is *specific* in function, whereas recycled junk was responsive to fantasy. (For a parallel consider the difference between radio and television. In the radio serial, you had to imagine what people looked like. You had to clothe them and create their landscapes. In television? Everything is pre-imagined. There is nothing left for a child to do.)

There were vogues for pump-action humming tops, marbles, bubble pipes, pea shooters, spud-guns, billy carts with screaming, ball-bearing wheels and completely illegal shanghais, where the rubber propellant was cut from your Dad's spare inner-tube. There were balsa-wood gliders, little wooden yachts that you took to Elwood beach and which steadfastly refused to sail, home-made bows and arrows and explosive devices created by packing the sulphur off matchheads into bolts for throwing at brick walls. For every Christmas or birthday toy actually purchased in a shop, there were ten that you made yourself. Like wooden stilts or jam-tin stilts with string attached. Like Jam-tin telephones, also with string attached. Then there were brown-paper kites that wouldn't fly, the discovery that you could burn holes in paper with a magnifying glass, the terrifying joy of pricking your finger with a compass so that you could write your name in blood . . . and the wonderment that one golf ball could contain approximately two miles of tightly wound rubber.

It was an era when toys were recycled, when you suffered the humiliation of the hand-me-down. Thus my first two-wheeler was an uncle's bike crudely repainted with old-fashioned red tyres that made me the laughing stock of the bike shed. But from the same source I got a broken-down air gun that was widely, wildly desired by my mates.

Clearly the child of the 1940s or the 1950s would have been stupefied by the toys of today. Even from our contemporary viewpoint, their ingenuity lies somewhere between the enthralling and the intimidating. Yet as I look at them they remind me of Aldous Huxley's assertion — that man has stopped evolving and that, instead, our machines are evolving for us. We have a new generation of toys that play with themselves, by themselves. They have no need of children.

Sugar and spice

I've just survived my youngest daughter's seventh birthday party. Sixteen demented dwarfs descended on the place, screaming pygmies in frilly dresses. The Lord of the Flies had nothing on these diminutive harridans and harpies. Tearing through the garden like a biblical plague, they left it looking like the most bombed and defoliated stretches of the Ho Chi Minh Trail. I managed to drive them back with cans of aerosol fly spray, but when they saw the food they were uncontrollable. Cakes, cocktail frankfurts, sausage rolls and potato crisps went everywhere. Into ears, eyes and up noses as well as mouths. Within seconds every child was smeared with tomato sauce and hydrophobic with cream. It was even scarier than the trailer for *Piranha II*, the new horror film in which a hybrid version of the aquatic carnivores takes wing.

I've seen lots of monsters over the years — men metamorphosing into werewolves, great lumbering brutes stitched together from dead bodies, killer vegetables from outer space (e.g. the Triffids and the Thing), not to mention blobs, godzillas, sharks, rampaging bull ants and creatures from black lagoons. But they were *nothing* beside the horrifying onslaught of sixteen seven-year-old girls. Even though heavily sedated, I know I'll wake up screaming from nightmares.

Little boys, we were told, are made from snips and snails and puppy dogs' tails. Whereas little girls are sugar, spice and everything nice. Whoever wrote those lyrics should be sued or pilloried. Better still, we should have invited him to the party.

Towards the end of the day I was hanging banners on the front fence saying 'Collect one, get one free'. However, parents showed an understandable reluctance to return. It took phone calls, threats and entreaties until almost all of them were collected. I was just tying the left-over balloons to the left-over child, so that I could launch her over the rotary clothes line and the roof, when the last father arrived. I was happy to pay him the ransom money.

Sugar and spice indeed. That bunch are all destined to grow up into Margaret Thatchers, Imelda Marcoses and Madam Gandhis.

The all-seeing Patrick White

Being allergic to social occasions, whether imposing or intimate, I'm notorious for declining invitations to openings, launchings, cocktails, birthdays and dinner parties. But when James and Freda McClelland invited me to meet Patrick White, the one human being whom I still regarded with reverence and awe, I RSVP'd as eagerly as a novice offered a papal audience.

No, it wasn't *the* dinner party described in White's autobiography when the McClellands had also invited the Kerrs, 'the Macbeths of Yarralumla'. Apart from Patrick and Manoly, the other guests would be the far more distinguished Jean Battersby and Nugget Coombs. Thus I approached the event — and the McClellands' front door — with trepidation.

By this time in my life, I'd met innumerable notables: a pride of PMs, an eddy of editors, a tedium of telly stars, a sell-out of celebrities, a cretinue of critics. All in all, a disenchanting experience as most of your larger-than-lifers turned out to be, well, merely human. Even the illustrious internationals I'd met (including presidential candidates, five mega-stars and a consumer crusader) had had their frailties. Deities with dandruff. Flaws in the glass.

And while it was immature to expect the mighty to be more than mortal, it was sad to find so many of one's heroes were more like garden gnomes than the classic statues you'd expected. In many a great man's shoes I discovered both odd socks and feet of clay.

Patrick White would, though, be different. He was not simply a man but the tree of man. Despising his fame and transcending politics he was that mountain among mole hills, a Great Writer.

Yet what I met was a supercilious, fastidious man who, for some reason, reminded me of the last Empress of China. Not that I knew her well, but there was the same imperial aloofness, an ineffable sense of aristocracy. Though seated beside us at the table, White seemed to be enthroned. Haughty and prim-mouthed, he gazed down at us with a sort of quizzical indifference.

When we were introduced, White dismissed me with the following words: 'I don't understand your articles'. Mind you there wasn't the slightest curiosity in the remark. Whereas I'd struggled to comprehend his works he hadn't the slightest interest in mine. On another level, his comment was decidedly incongruous, tantamount to the world's greatest cryptologist confessing to an ignorance of the simplest morse or semaphore.

But then, this indifference seemed to extend to everything and everybody. It was as if White was as old as Grendel's dragon, and that his all-seeing and all-knowing had cursed him with a fathomless boredom. Throughout the evening he seemed always on the verge of stifling a yawn.

Far from resenting his aloofish loftiness, I was transfixed. Where any number of famous giants had turned out to be pygmies, White was an outrageous overstatement. The first time I'd read his work I realised that he was homosexual (and always puzzled why earnest academic analyses avoided the issue) and here he was behaving like Lady Bracknell in *The Importance of Being Earnest*. I refer, of course, to the immortal interpretation by Martita Hunt.

When I asked Patrick why he'd given up travelling, he simply shrugged. He'd been everywhere, seen everything and, in any case, the world had been ruined by recent vulgarities. He preferred to revisit favourite places in his mind — just as he does in an odyssey around the Greek islands, oddly appended to *Flaws in the Glass*. And in any case, there was the cinema.

Whereupon he and Nugget began having an argument about the value of colour in movies. Patrick was all for the joys of polychrome, whereas Nugget felt that black and white was infinitely superior. It pared cinema down to its essentials, allowed a more elemental presentation of ideas. But not for Patrick. Very much the voluptuary, he wanted to wallow in the visual experience.

When they got down to discussing specific films, it suddenly emerged that Nugget saw films in black and white even when they weren't. A couple of favourite films that had rainbowed memories for the rest of us were monochrome for him. (Good heavens! The boss of the Reserve Bank was colour blind! Well, that obviously enhanced his abilities to be an advocate for Australia's blacks, but it made you wonder how he got on when he was signing all the bank notes.)

For a while I found White infuriating in the faint amusement, nudging contempt, that he felt for almost everyone and everything discussed. Leaving aside his endorsement for Eastman colour. Yet after a while I recognised that his indifference derived from both weariness and pain. He had a quality that I've subsequently observed in a number of the wealthiest and most powerful men in the country — an absence of self-delusion. Indeed, his constant analysis of motive and meaning had produced self-hatred. As anyone reading *Flaws in the Glass* will know, while White can be very bitter about other people, he's totally unforgiving about himself.

As the evening progressed I tried hard to like White, something he makes as difficult as possible. Clearly he's embarrassed by praise, suspicious of friendship and, really, doesn't *like* to be liked. In the end, however, you do like him, if only because he just doesn't give a damn.

Thinking about him afterwards, and after ten years the meeting remains vivid in my memory where a million others have faded completely, I still see the last Empress of China on the one hand and the tree of man on the other. White is cursed with seeing everything far, far too clearly. And that everything includes, indeed begins with, himself.

The second time I met Patrick he'd been named Australian of the Year and had shocked the organiser by announcing his intention of hacking the medal into three bits — so that he could give one bit to his satiric doppelganger, Barry Humphries, and the other to the extraordinary Jack Mundy. White was flying down from Sydney for a function at the

Melbourne Town Hall and Barry Jones and I had agreed to collect him at the airport.

We waited in the concourse while the people piled through the door. We waited and we waited. No sign of Patrick. Had he decided, at the last moment, to snub the event? That would be quite consistent with his attitudes. Far more consistent than accepting the award. But just when we were turning away to go and phone the organisers, there he was. He'd been stuck right down the back of the plane.

Consider that for a moment. Australia's Nobel-Prize-winning author and the Australian of the Year. The organisers had bought him a second-class ticket! There was something so marvellously incongruously Australian about it. Egalitarianism run riot. You organise something as preposterous as an Australian of the Year Award and give it to someone as dangerous as White and then insult him by plonking him in 27F. Not that anyone at the airline would have had the brains to upgrade him. Patrick who?

When we dropped him back at Tulla a few hours later, I upgraded him to first class myself. Not that Patrick had complained about it. He would have regarded it as appropriately symbolic of the way the artist had been treated in this country for many, many years. As Barry Jones pointed out at the time, the Queen had knighted far more of our jockeys than she had our writers or painters.

Another White story that I cannot personally verify. But I've heard it from a few different sources and it *feels* true, even if it's apocryphal. It concerns the historic first meeting of Patrick White with Frank Hardy.

Now, it's probably true that Frank regards himself as Patrick's equal. Indeed, I've heard suggestions that he thinks that White got *his* Nobel Prize. So over the years it's alleged that Frank has nursed a literary grievance.

Then, one night in Sydney, Hardy arrived at a posh restaurant feeling somewhat tired and emotional. As he stepped through the door he saw, at a distant table, Patrick dining with Manoly. The first reaction was teeth-gnashing rage. There he was — the pretender to Hardy's throne. But Frank is, as anyone will tell you, a civilised sort of chap. So he decided to let bygones by bygones and to introduce himself. Whereupon the author of *Power Without Glory*, *The Four Legged Lottery* and *The Dead Are Many* began to weave his way across the restaurant towards the author of *The Aunt's Story*, *The Solid Mandala*, *Riders in the Chariot* and *Voss*. Finally he reached the table and thrust out his hand. 'Patrick White', he said, 'Frank Hardy!'

Patrick stopped eating. Put his knife and fork down. Looked up at Frank for a few silent seconds. And then a man who has a great command of the English language blew Hardy a long, loud, wet raspberry.

The courtesy of Coward

The literary world was both shocked and delighted when Patrick White sank the slipper in *Flaws in the Glass*. The Duke of Edinburgh and Sirs John Kerr and Sid Nolan were amongst the galaxy of stars to feel the toe-cap of our Nobel laureate. But when you read how Noel Coward put in the boot, you see that Patrick was merely playing footsie.

In the diary Coward kept between 1941 and 1969 (now edited by Graham Payne and Robert Morley's industrious son, Sheridan), we learn that the playwright was *for* the death penalty, the monarchy and the Conservative Party whilst being *against* the prosecution of homosexuals. He was also against almost everybody else.

Arthur Miller was dismissed as boring and embarrassing.

Graham Greene was rated 'tedious, pretentious, most unpleasant'.

Poor Tennessee Williams, for whom one might have expected Coward to feel a certain sexual camaraderie, was 'intolerable'.

The beautiful Lili Palmer was *not* a favourite leading lady: 'I have never worked with such a stupid bitch'.

Slow, pompous and obstructive, was Coward's critique of Michael Redgrave.

Christine Keeler and Mandy Rice-Davies were 'miserable little tarts'.

As for the Beatles, they were 'talentless, bad-mannered little shits'.

It was only when he approached the upper echelons that Coward dropped a verbal curtsy. Suddenly nasty Noel became the lap dog, a sort of human Corgi. Thus, throughout the journals, the Royal family are full of 'radiance'.

Yet I'm willing to forgive him everything for one devastating punchline. Coward visited the Old Vic. to watch Vivien Leigh play Lavinia in Shakespeare's grim little number, *Titus Andronicus*, which is more or less the *Mad Max II* of the Bard's output. It was, I believe, the only play presented at the Globe with an R certificate. The role of Lavinia offers an actress an interesting technical challenge as, for much of the goings-on, she can communicate only through tears. This is because her tongue is cut out, and her hands amputated, by the wicked Demetrius and Chiron who have ravished her.

Things reach a sort of climax when Lavinia attempts to identify her violators by writing their names in the sand, using a stick grasped between her forearms. Unfortunately, at this critical moment, Miss Leigh dropped the stick, causing no end of confusion amongst her fellow actors.

Whereupon Coward cried out: 'Butter stumps!'

Hitler is still around

In a world where kids have never heard of Humbers, hubba-hubba and Hoyts' matinees, it should come as no surprise that Hitler seems as remote as Hannibal. Insofar as Nazis are known, they're the funny characters in the umpteenth re-run of Hogan's Heroes.

Well, if Hitler were still around (an old-age pensioner in the Argentine?) he'd be ninety-four.

Irrespective of his state of health, Hitler's beliefs are alive and kicking and not just in the minds of octogenarian Nazis in their South American hideaways. All too often one hears echoes of his ideology in the statements of incipient totalitarians. And not just in sleazy dictatorships of the military or the proletariat but in respectable western societies threatened by rising social tensions and by men who believe it's time to talk commonsense about over-education, under-employment and social discipline.

Isn't there a chance that Sir Oswald Mosley would be welcomed in today's Britain? Certainly there are men to the right of Reagan who grow impatient with the self-indulgences of democracy, recalling Hitler's ironic observations that 'the great strength of the totalitarian state is that it forces those who fear it to imitate it'.

Consider the modern election as candidates jostle to be premiers, presidents or prime ministers. In their strategies and tactics, you find echoes of the führer's philosophy of propaganda.

'The size of the lie is a definite factor in causing it to be believed, for the vast masses of a nation are in the depths of their hearts more easily deceived than they are consciously and intentionally bad. The primitive simplicity of their minds renders them a more easy prey to a big lie than a small one.

'All propaganda must be so popular and on such an intellectual level, that even the most stupid of those towards whom it is directed will understand it. Therefore the intellectual level of the propaganda must be lower, the larger the number of people who are to be influenced by it.

'Through clever and constant application of propaganda, people can be made to see Paradise as Hell, and also the other way round, to consider the most wretched sort of life as Paradise.

'The receptive ability of the great masses is only very limited, their understanding is small. On the other hand, their forgetfulness is great. This being so, all effective propaganda should be limited to very few points which, in turn, should be used as slogans until even the very last man is able to imagine what is meant.'

Speaking of slogans, Hitler was a great one for tossing off the memorable one-liner. 'Hate is more lasting than dislike.' 'The victor will never be asked if he told the truth.' 'A great politician has to bother himself less with means than with the goal.' 'Success is the sole earthly judge of right and wrong.' 'Humanitarianism is the expression of stupidity and cowardice.'

Were he active today, he'd certainly prefer the electronic media to newspapers or magazines. The master of political theatricality would want the direct access to the populace that the telly, like the mass rally, provides. 'All epoch-making revolutionary events have been produced not by the written but by the spoken word.'

While Hitler would have modified his techniques in using network ratings rather than Nuremburg rallies, he'd have relied on the irrationality of the mass audience. The lump in the throat created by, for example, the opening of Joh's Commonwealth Games would be magnified by a Hitler who shared the vulgar vision of a deMille.

'At a mass meeting thought is eliminated and because this is the state of mind I require, because it secures to me the best sounding board for my speeches, I order everyone to attend the meeting, where they become part of a mass whether they like it or not. "Intellectuals" and bourgeois as well as workers.'

Like many modern leaders, Hitler found the press an irritation. There's hardly a politician on the planet who hasn't, at times, dreamed of doing exactly what Hitler did to troublesome journalists. 'The organisation of our press is such that divergences of opinion between members of the government are no longer an occasion for public exhibition, which are not the newspapers' business. We have eliminated that conception of political freedom which holds that everybody has the right to say whatever comes into his head.'

More and more you hear people saying that education is wasted on the dunderheads of society, that it gives them greater expectations than society can hope to fulfil.

'Universal education is the most corroding and disintegrating poison that liberalism has ever invented for its own destruction', said the führer. At the same time, he saw his uneducated Alfs as providing the necessary muscle. 'A violently active, dominating, intrepid, brutal youth — that is what I'm after. I want to see in its eyes the gleam of pride and independence, of prey. I have no intellectual training. Knowledge is ruined in my young men. I am liberating man from the degrading chimera known as conscience.'

Conscience? Not when 'natural instincts bid all living human beings not merely to conquer their enemies but also to destroy them'.

'The whole end of education', Hitler said, 'is found in burning into the hearts and brains of the youth an instinctive and comprehended sense of race ... The very first essential for success is a constant and regular employment of violence. The greatness of every mighty organisation ... lies in the religious fanaticism and intolerance with which it imposes its will against all others.'

Equality and democracy were, in Hitler's view, despicable concepts. 'The Jew always talks about the equality of all men, without regard of race and colour. Those who are idiots begin to believe that ... Democracy, the deceitful theory that the Jew would insinuate — naming that theory that all men are created equal. The one means that wins the easiest victory over reason: terror and force.

'We do not intend to abolish the inequality of man; on the contrary, we would deepen it and, as in ancient great civilisations, create insurmountable barriers which would turn it into law. There will be an historical class tempered by battle, and welded from the most varied elements. There will be a great hierarchy of party members. There will be the new middle class. And there will be the great mass of the anonymous, the serving collective, the eternally disenfranchised. Beneath them will be the class of subject alien races — we need not hesitate to call them the modern slave class.'

Despite John Bennett's revisionism, Hitler felt no qualms at the thought of genocide. 'If I can send the flower of the German nation into the hell of war without the smallest pity for the spilling of precious German blood, then surely I have the right to remove millions of an inferior race that breeds like vermin.'

(Emphatic on all matters, Hitler was also an uncompromising art critic. 'Anyone who sees and paints a sky green and pastures blue ought to be sterilised.')

These days the world abounds with little Hitlers, with

religious fanatics and ideologues who faithfully employ his tactics. Even in our own society, where the divisions between the classes, the sort of divisions that propelled his demagoguery, are deepening. It would be absurdly over-dramatic to say that there are potential führers in Australia, but clearly we've one or two provincial figures with their fantasies.

The real danger probably comes from the most ruthless pragmatists who are willing, like Hitler, to say things they *don't* believe in the interests of power. For of all the things Hitler said, I found the most ominous a throw-away line about the Jews. Words which implied that he didn't believe what he said about them, that anti-semitism was quite consciously chosen as the biggest of his Big Lies.

'Anti-semitism is a useful revolutionary expedient. My Jews are a valuable hostage given to me by democracy.'

The unstoppable Zsa Zsa

The phone rings. STD blips. Hello, this is the Parkinson programme. Would you, could you fly up next week and do the show? Having done two Parkinsons already, I ask who's died, fallen through or been banned by Actors' Equity. No, no, it isn't like that. Mike wanted you for the last taping of the series — and as it's with Zsa Zsa you might find it amusing.

Zsa Zsa, born Sari Gabor, Budapest 1919. Miss Hungary of 1936 who made her Hollywood debut in *Lovely to Look At* in 1952. Her brief cinematic career included a walk-on in Orson Welles's *Touch of Evil* in 1958, while in 1959 she was crowned Queen of Outer Space. Her only really significant part was in Huston's *Moulin Rouge* where she played the singer Jean Avril, and I suggest an appropriate clip.

What would I like to talk about? Well, in honour of Miss Gabor, perhaps I should discuss the mummification processes of the ancient Egyptians. I could bring my favourite mummy with me, that of Tabes, a 25th dynasty singer. We could then compare the comparative states of preservation of these two venerable showbiz personalities. The Parkinson people feel this might be just a little provocative and suggest that I natter about the International Year of the Disabled Person.

A few days later, a message is relayed from Miss Gabor at the Sebel Town House. Will I join her and her cousin for dinner? As I'm tired of being tossed like a frisbee between Tullamarine and Mascot, I gracefully decline. So I don't meet the dear lady until an hour before the taping at Channel 10. By now I've warmed to her a little, simply because of the way she's been attacked by our female journalists.

Having skinned poor Parky alive a few weeks earlier, the Melbourne *Herald*'s Tess Lawrence goes after Zsa Zsa in a page headed 'BLAH BLAH GABOR'. According to Tess, the Parkinson programme is such a ratings disaster that they're forced to prop it up by exploiting an unhealthy interest in this antique courtesan. An unhealthy interest that Tess herself proceeds to exploit, as only she can. By the end of the column, Miss Gabor has been carved up like a chicken: legs, breast and thighs all over the page. But is this entirely fair? From what one understands, Gabor, like Lawrence, is a woman making her way in the world of media, not pretending to be anything more than a professional celebrity.

While awaiting Sari's arrival, Mike and I chat over coffee. He discusses his difficulties with the press (the tall poppy syndrome), his relationship with Rupert Murdoch (still cordial), possible changes to the next series (minor). As usual, I find Mike enormously likeable and devoid of pretension. But he's obviously delighted to be taping the last show.

Now I'm called into make-up and, as my skin blemishes are buried beneath three coats of Max Factor, I hear a discussion of Zsa Zsa's dress. 'She says she paid $3,000 for it', says a lady from Costumes. 'And it's absolute *rubbish*. The stitching's awful, the whole thing's falling apart. They really con these stars. Just because they'd pay lots of money for it in Beverly Hills, they think it has to be good.'

'Yes, Peter Allen was saying that he spends $100 on a hair cut. You could get just as good a job for $5.'

'Mind you, *her* stitches are holding together pretty well.'

'Yes, better than the dress's.'

On the set, I'm suddenly confronted by Zsa Zsa, with her high cheekbones, pinched nostrils and hair in curlers. 'Hello dollink', she says, 'but you mustn't look at me. I'm looking just so *ghastly*!'

Along with everyone else on the set, I feel obliged to reassure her as to her astonishing pulchritude. 'Which is my camera, dollink?' she enquires of the floor manager. 'Camera two, Miss Gabor.' She rushes to the cameraman and says 'I want *very* high angles. Please put your camera up as high as it will go.' A hundred per cent professional, Zsa Zsa knows that high angles hide double chins. She checks the lighting set-up and seems satisfied.

A few minutes later, Zsa Zsa reappears in the $3,000 dress, a vivid green number with a sort of cabbage on the left shoulder. This cloth corsage is artfully designed to prevent close-ups of her neck and shoulders, where the skin is showing its mileage.

By the time the audience fills the seats and the technicians have everything under control, we've had ample opportunity to assess the lady. There is no detectable difference between the persona and the person. The performance is non-stop — lots of dollinks, giggles and an almost complete indifference to what is happening around her. She hardly seems to notice other human beings. It's her hair that matters, the way her $3,000 dress fits, the way her make-up looks. (She uses a studio monitor with the same familiarity as another woman might her compact mirror.) And when the interview begins, she tells her time-worn anecdotes about George Sanders, Nicky Hilton, Jack Kennedy and the rest as she's told them a thousand times before. Yet she has pleasure in telling them, and laughs at her little jokes as though she'd just thought of them. Mike has very little to do except sit back while Gabor gossips, and the picture that emerges is not entirely unattractive.

While she obfuscates about her age, that's a part of the act, the only area where she bothers to pretend about anything. She has one topic of conversation, herself. (Two topics, if you include jewellery.) The only problem is that she finds it impossible to *stop* talking and keeps prattling away during the commercial breaks, talking to Mike, to the crew and to the audience without ever waiting for a reply.

Then it's my turn to lumber down the stairs. Needing to concentrate on Parkinson, I sit with my back towards the still chattering celebrity. (I'll get a lot of hate mail over this, but it was done in desperation rather than rudeness.) The second that she ceases to be the centre of interest, Zsa Zsa complains, saying 'Vot am I doink here dollink? Why don't I go?' And when dear old David Bellamy joins us, she infuriates Parkinson by chattering to me *throughout* his impassioned speech about Australian fauna. She literally *never* stops talking, thoroughly unsettling Parkinson. If looks could kill, they'd be rushing Zsa Zsa to the Coroner's Court and Parkinson would be up on charges.

As we're off camera during Bellamy's chat, I try to quieten Zsa Zsa down. Too energetic to be thrown, Bellamy determinedly rhapsodises over Banksias. During the next break Zsa Zsa, who doesn't seem to have noticed Bellamy's presence, is still talking nineteen to the dozen, telling Mike that she wants to plug the Varatah National Park and their lovely Colas (i.e. Cola Bears). Blazing with anger, he tells her that she is *not*, positively not to do this. Yet as soon as the little red light appears on the camera, this impervious lady announces her undying love for those dollink little Colas, while Parkinson's knuckles whiten on his arm rests. Zsa Zsa feigns a Monroesque vagueness when it suits her. She crashes through all objections, like a scented, foam-rubber Centurion tank.

Fascinated by Bellamy's missionary zeal, I take on the role of chlorophyllip and turn the conversation back to Banksias, ferns and rain forests. But words continue to gush from Zsa Zsa like oil from a ruptured well. And I doubt that even a Red Adair could stop the flow.

After the programme, when Michael would clearly like to run her down with a camera dolly, Zsa Zsa calls everybody dollink and gives us brisk pecks on the cheek. The last time I see her, she's sweeping off to make-up, somehow reminding me of Turner's magnificent painting, 'The Return of the Golden Hind'.

Parkinson, who's lost almost a stone during the series, looks absolutely buggered. He has just survived ninety minutes with the tyrannosaurus rex of talk shows. And as she disappears down the corridor, she is still talking, talking, talking. And the staff and crew shake their heads in disbelief and wonderment.

'Do you know how old she *really* is?' says an effeminate member of her entourage through clenched teeth. 'Sixty-five.'

Just as Frank Thring embodies a vanished form of theatricality, a now irrelevant form of social provocation, Zsa Zsa threshes out a Hollywood fantasy. Like the mighty wurlitzers that upsurged in glittering, gold-leafed cinemas, we shall not see her like again.

Herpe days

How's this for a scoop: the Moral Majority are using biological warfare against unsuspecting sinners. A virulent form of herpes, a Biblical plague emanating from Sodom and Gomorrah, has been lovingly cultured for centuries in the crypts of cathedrals. Now the long-dormant disease has been released to provoke panic among the promiscuous, an outrage that demands the re-opening of the Nuremberg Trials.

As a result of this cruellest of culture shocks, detumescence is rampant if that's not a contradiction in terms. Only the bravest of lechers and sybarites are able to keep a stiff upper. The red lights are going out all over Europe and St Kilda Road and, just a few weeks back, Australian *Penthouse* took on the abandoned appearance of a burnt-out führer bunker.

Well, we concupiscent won't take this sort of thing standing up. We're determined to fight back, to give the herpes sufferer his or her self-regard. From now on the tell-tale cold sore will be worn as proudly as a duelling scar.

After all, the aristocracy of Europe learnt to live with syphilis. There was a time when it was as common amongst royal families as haemophilia (as a child studying French history I vividly recalled the description of one of the Louis removing his hose at night, only to find a few of his toes had dropped off). It became so common amongst the British nobility (e.g. Winston Churchill's father) that nobody thought anything much about it.

This contrasted with the appalling behaviour of earlier eras when, it seems, the spread of syphilis provoked the widespread burning of witches. Modern scholars are now convinced that Syph provoked such righteous indignation amongst the influential that they started barbecuing those branded as carriers. In a cruel and malodorous phenomenon that the Reverend Falwell would applaud, sexual suspects were incinerated by the thousand.

And that's what the Moral Majority would like to do with herpes sufferers. By designating the disease the leprosy of the lascivious they're trying to create a new cast of outcasts.

Which is why I volunteer to give my professional services free to the Herpes Institute. I'm quite convinced we can make the ailment socially acceptable, even imbuing it with a degree of glamour. At the end of my twelve months' campaign people *without* herpes will be feeling diffident, even apologetic. And with the passage of time, the herpes sore will be a status symbol, worn like a Rotary badge.

First we'll begin with an up-beat jingle called 'Herpe Days Are Here Again'.

> Herpe days are here again
> My upper lip's not clear again
> Let us sing a song of cheer again
> Herpe days are here again.

Then we'll be throwing a series of parties at which people

will celebrate their first infection. For these I'll be hiring the New Seekers to sing 'Herpe Birthday To You'. These bright, cheerful functions will be compered by that old trouper from Melbourne's Channel 7, Herpe Hammond.

Some of you may question the possibility of making an illness socially attractive. Well, let me refer you to the romantic glow that surrounded tuberculosis in the 19th century. As Susan Sontag observed in 'Illness as Metaphor' tuberculosis implied a poetic, sensitive sensibility and the popular arts were forever producing images of Camilles coughing into lace hankies, leaving telltale spots of blood. In more recent times magazines like the *Reader's Digest* have popularised a sort of Disneyfied version of Freud so that almost anyone who's anybody now boasts a neurosis and a psychiatrist. Indeed, in Manhattan and Los Angeles, the time one spends in analysis is at least as important as the holidays one enjoys at St Tropez.

So see you at our fund-raising screening at the Hoyts complex. We're running 'The Herpiest Days of Our Lives'.

Subtitles

In our multicultural, subtitled and Al Grassby world, we welcome ethnic diversity with cries of 'encore' and 'olé'. No longer inhibited cheddar nibblers, we reel from the deli loaded with Goudas, Edams and Roquefort crying 'What a friend we have in cheeses!' While not despising our sturdy lagers, we now quaff a plethora of plonks, boasting of vintages that mimic the vineyards of Europe. And while the sight of a mint-condition FJ can still exhilarate an Australian autophile, our Renaults, Volvos, Peugeots and Alfa Romeos proclaim our global view.

But things were clearly different and far more provincial in the golden age of Hollywood when it was de rigueur to change one's foreign-sounding name to something cute for the marquee. You'll remember that, when immigrants arrived at Ellis Island, belligerent bureaucrats simply couldn't be bothered writing down those polysyllabic names, characterised by an excess of consonants over vowels, and simply issued people with new ones. Well, it was much the same at the Los Angeles studios where truly magnificent appellations were reduced to human brandnames with an emphasis on the alliterative. I don't know what Mickey Mouse's real name was but Diana Dors and Doris Day were, originally, Diana Fluck and Doris Kappelhoff.

But perhaps the moguls weren't being racist so much as energy-conscious. After all, putting Issur Danielovitch Demsky or Maria Magdalena Von Losch up in lights would be far, far more expensive than shining out Kirk Douglas and Marlene Dietrich. Quite apart from the power bills, think of the saving on globes. (I really must have a fatherly chat with Angela Punch-McGregor. It's costing me a *fortune* to give her top billing in *We of the Never Never*.)

In many cases, there was no attempt to Anglicise the name — it was just that the original was considered too elaborate, too fruity. Yet would Clifton Webb's career have been less distinguished had he remained Webb Parmelee Hollenbeck? Surely the name is superior to that of his best-loved character, Mr Belvedere. Mind you, Mr Hollenbeck might have been daunted by the thought of autograph hunters: imagine writing Webb Parmelee Hollenbeck 500 times at the première of *Three Coins in the Fountain.*

The penchant for alliteration that turned Camille Javal into Brigitte Bardot didn't save Shirley Schrift from getting short shrift in Hollywood. Clearly it was easier to say Shelley Winters with ill-fitting dentures. But why turn Raquel Tejada into Raquel Welch? Tejada has a certain mystery to it whereas Welch is the verbal counterpart to a pickled onion. And what's the sense of turning Peggy Middleton into Yvonne De Carlo when, conversely, Anna Maria Italiano was rechristened Anne Bancroft?

Would the films of Fred Astaire and Ginger Rogers have been less successful had they starred Frederick Austerlitz and Virginia McMath? Would Mickey Rooney have been diminished if he'd remained Joe Yule Jr? And surely Ray Milland would have been as convincing a cad or bounder if he'd kept Reginald Truscott Jones?

OK, John Wayne could hardly go around calling himself Marion Michael Morrison and Jeff Chandler's long career playing Indian chiefs might have been inhibited had he remained Ira Grossel. And I'll concede that Cyd Charisse trips off the tongue better than Tula Ellice Finklea. But don't tell me that Robert Taylor wouldn't have melted as many hearts as Spangler Arlington Brugh.

And I can't see why the effervescent and bubbling Busby Berkeley didn't stay with *his* original name, William Berkeley Enos. Enos. You can't be much more bubbly and effervescent than *that*.

Was it anti-semitism or unpronounceability that persuaded two generations of Jewish comedians to adopt Christian names? Allen Konigsberg to Woody Allen. Benjamin Kubelsky to Jack Benny. Mendel Berlinger to Milton Berle. Melvin Kaminsky to Mel Brooks. Nathan Birnbaum to George Burns. Judith Tuvim to Judy Holliday. David Daniel Kaminsky to Danny Kaye.

What's *unforgivable* is the fact that W.C. Fields began life as William Claude Dukinfield which, on any criteria, is a far funnier name. Indeed, William Claude Dukinfield is right up there with some of the concoctions of Groucho Marx — like Captain Hackenbush. I'd go so far as to say that it's comparable with the immortal Jubilation T. Cornpone.

Joan Crawford? She was christened Lucille le Sueur so you can understand her leaping on an alias. Frances Gumm was probably too earth-bound to soar over the rainbow while John Pringle sounds more like the editor of the *Sydney Morning Herald* than the movie star, John Gilbert. And if le Sueur was an unfortunate appellation, what about Vilma Lonchit? Not that the substitute surname of Banky is all that alluring.

Anyway, the same practice is catching on here in Australia. While some in this subtitled, Al Grassby world are trying to climb on the multicultural bandwagon (film identities Joe Skrzynski, Fred Schepisi and Igor Auzins were originally named Arthur Briggs, Fred Clarke and Bob Smith), I'm able to reveal that Bryan Brown's real name is Montague Pauncefoot, that Jack Thompson came into the world as Spencer Prognose and that Helen Morse was christened Gladys Pforzheimer. Kate Fitzpatrick has rejected her real name (Mildred Bignorks) and Judy Davis no longer answers to Fiona Bromo-Fewsdale. And that's the truth, as sure as *my* name is Yoxall Exelby Ffoulkes.

Vice-Regal vices

The former Premier of South Australia, Mr Don Dunstan, said today he had been 'surprised' by a letter Sir Doug Nicholls had written to him warning of the dangers of appointing a white man as Governor.

The letter warned that the appointment of a honky could lead to Government House being filled with boring members of the Adelaide Establishment and their gushy, over-dressed wives. There would also be a tendency for social-climbing businessmen to inveigle their way into the premises in the hope of obtaining MBEs, OBEs and knighthoods. Once the Liberals were returned to power.

Worse still, Sir Douglas warned that a pale face might bring vice back into Vice-Regal circles. Unfortunately the Premier's office ignored the letter and Sir Douglas's prophecies were fulfilled.

Mind you, it could have been worse. At least the present incumbent of Adelaide's Government House is an Australian. The *real* problem was with the Poms that Buck. Palace sends to the colonies, usually to dispose of political embarrassments at Whitehall. Apart from their notorious tendency to avoid regular ablutions, British-born Governors have been, since the Rum Rebellion, a rum lot.

While stressing that I'm not a racist, my allegiance to objectivity in journalism forces me to reveal that, amongst Victoria's recent Governors of British origin, we've had one who was guilty of financial shenanigans and the grand larceny of a number of important paintings. This was revealed to me (scout's honour) by the aide-de-camp of a more recent, more honourable incumbent.

He described his Guv's first night as host to the Melbourne gentry — at a dinner in the enormous dining room that *infuriated* Queen Victoria. (For the simple reason that Melbourne's grand-standing land boomers had *dared* to build one larger than hers at Buckingham Palace.) As His Excellency stood at the door shaking hands with a who's who of the socially prominent, he was puzzled by the number of white envelopes that were pressed into his palm. Muttering 'thank you's' he kept stuffing them in his inside pocket, assuming they were letters of welcome. A little later in the evening, he opened one to discover it was stuffed with bank notes. As were the others!

Mystified by this munificence, the Governor made enquiries and was *horrified* to discover that his predecessor was in the habit of *charging*. Needing extra money for the neddies, he'd let it be known that guests were expected to cough up.

Then there was the Case of the Missing Paintings. A popular Governor of Victoria was wont to ring up the National Gallery to borrow the odd example of the Heidelberg School. Over the years the walls of Government House were enhanced by any number of McCubbins, Withers and such like. The Governor became so attached to these charming daubs that he packed them in his suitcases on his departure and it was only after protracted correspondence with an excruciatingly embarrassed Victorian Government that they were returned. So much for Sir Mark Oliphant's anxiety about Aboriginal house-guests and the 'loss of valuables'.

Not that all our British-born Vice-Regals have been lightfingered. But one recent incumbent was, to say the least, eccentric. I revealed the following story some years ago only to find most readers convinced it was apocryphal. Just another piece of Adams whimsy. Not so. It was just a prime example of reality surpassing satire.

While visiting the elegant white building in Melbourne's Botanic Gardens, I was allowed to peek inside Sir Rohan 'Jumbo' Delacombe's private quarters. And there, in his bedroom, was a vast collection of inflatable vinyl animals. It was like a pneumatic version of Tennessee Williams's *Glass Menagerie*. They dangled from the bedpost and the chandelier, bobbed in the armchair and were pushed listlessly around the floor by the draught. 'Oh my God', said the aide-de-camp, 'his seal's gone all puckered.' Whereupon he rushed to a deflated amphibian and gave it mouth-to-valve resuscitation.

Out of discretion, I waited until Sir Rohan had departed our shores before revealing his extraordinary fetish. But nobody, it seemed, was willing to believe me.

Sir Marcus Oliphant warned that an Aboriginal Governor could lead to Government House being filled with Aboriginal relatives. But what about a British Governor filling the Vice-Regal accommodations with polychromed inflatables? God, it's tantamount to learning that Sir Zelman Cowan is president of the Elvis Presley fan club and chairs meetings of the Executive Council in a tu-tu.

All in all, we've had some rather odd Poms in our ostrich plumes.

> **THE BIGGEST BANG IN THE COMMUNICATIONS EXPLOSION!**
>
> **SUPERSEDING CINEMA, RADIO, TELEVISION, THE VIDEO CASSETTE *AND* THE VIDEO DISC!**
>
> **INTRODUCING THE PRINT CARTRIDGE!***
>
> (*Otherwise known as 'The Book'.)

Check out the amazing advantages!

The Print Cartridge needs no batteries, operates without AC or DC current. It's fully portable — you can take a Print Cartridge anywhere.

Amazing Technical Features!

Fast forward! Flick through the pages at thousands of words a minute! Exclusive word search facility! Simply use your finger to pick out a favourite noun, verb or adjective! Remember that Print Cartridges offer you Freeze Page! And you can re-read your favourite bits over and over again!

An unbeatable array of titles!

Blasts from the past! Contemporary themes! Science fiction! Literally millions of Print Cartridges are already in stock. And they're available in all languages!

Huge savings on video cassettes!
Instead of outlaying $70 on a video disc of *Breakfast at Tiffany's* or *War and Peace*, read the original for as little as $4.95!

Experience amazing pictures inside your head!
Fantastic reproduction ... does not disturb people in the same room!

Fully compatible!
Unlike video cassettes which are unplayable on the wrong machine, Print Cartridges (or Paper Cassettes) can be enjoyed by anyone irrespective of their size or shape! All you need is a reasonable standard of literacy.

Fully portable!
Carry them anywhere! No special replay system required! Enjoy them everywhere you go — in bed, on the bus, on the loo!

Complete programme choice!
Everyone in the room can view their own paper cartridge simultaneously!

Skip over boring bits at will!
Re-read interesting or spicy bits over and over again!

Totally silent in operation!
Not affected by airport x-rays! Guaranteed foolproof! No after sales service required!

No danger of being superseded by a new technology!
Print Cartridges have been proven in laboratory experiments over hundreds of years. First developed by mediaeval monks with recent improvements by Gutenberg and Caxton! If you're sick of pictures, feast your eyes on restful words!

Hundreds of new titles constantly available!
Do-it-yourself! Self-improvement! Gardening, politics, languages, pornography!

Blank Paper Cartridges are also available for recording purposes!
They take pencil, biro or crayon!

Record your own thoughts and impressions!
Doodle or draw! And remember that Paper Cartridges use less energy, cut down on electricity bills.

Yes, Paper Cassettes and Print Cartridges are the new, modern, with-it way to blow your mind!
Exciting stories about white whales, Christmas ghosts, spectacular Russian wars! Go 20,000 leagues beneath the sea with Jules Verne or fly to Mars with Ray Bradbury! You've seen the movie and watched the mini-series — now read the Paper Cassette!

And remember, Paper Cassettes are *not* interrupted by TV commercials.

TAKE A LOOK AT A BOOK! (Copyright, patent pending.) NOW AVAILABLE WITH EXCLUSIVE SLOW-MOTION — READ THEM ALOUD, ONE WORD AT A TIME! DWELL ON ONE PAGE FOR AGES AND AGES! ONLY PAPER CASSETTES GIVE YOU THIS AMAZING FLEXIBILITY! AND REMEMBER, WHILE YOU CAN PURCHASE PRINT CARTRIDGES OUTRIGHT AT SHOPS AND NEWSAGENTS, THERE'S NO NEED TO BUY! *BORROW THEM* FROM PRINT CARTRIDGE CENTRES, OTHERWISE KNOWN AS LIBRARIES.

Limp or stiff! High brow or low brow! Instead of closing your mind, open some covers *today*.

STOP PRESS:

PRINT CARTRIDGES ARE DIGITAL!
That is, they are typed with digits.

Confessions of a TV critic

Television is chewing gum for the eyes, said John Mason Brown. It's for being on, not looking at, said Noel Coward. It is a medium of entertainment which permits millions of people to listen to the same joke at the same time, and yet remain lonesome, observed T.S. Eliot.

Malcolm Muggeridge observed that 'television was not intended to make human beings vacuous, but it is an emanation of their vacuity'. And J.B. Priestley believed that 'we viewers, when not viewing, have begun to whisper to one another, that the more we elaborate our means of communication, the less we communicate'.

Someone called Harriet Van Horne complained that there were 'days when any electrical appliance in the house, including the vacuum cleaner, seemed to offer more entertainment possibilities than the TV set'. And that sad self-parody, that left-over leviathan, Orson Welles, confessed to hating television 'as much as peanuts. But I can't stop eating peanuts.'

Well, I've been writing about television on and off for twenty years. During ten years spent as TV critic for the *Australian*, I formulated Adams's First Law of Television which holds that 'The weight of the backside is greater than the force of intellect'. (Mind you, that observation has been rendered redundant by the invention of the remote control.) And on the 15th anniversary of telly, I said: 'We haven't had fifteen years of television, but one year's television fifteen times'.

Now let me confess. Let me make a clean breast of it. The truth is I *love* television. I think it's the most maligned, insulted and libelled of appliances. Idiot box? Boob tube? Nonsense. The television set is a paragon of electrical virtues, the greatest contributor to human wellbeing since the invention of the toaster. I know it's true because, right at the moment, I'm suffering from withdrawal symptoms as, one by one, my favourite programmes fade to black.

While the religious torments of aristocratic, English homosexuals are as remote from my experience as the circumcision rituals of the Hottentots, here is one atheistic, working class, Australian hetero who was entranced by *Brideshead Revisited*. To hell with the characters. Any excuse to perve on the interiors of stately homes and Venetian palaces will be gratefully accepted by me. I loved the ratbaggery of Ryder's father, so impeccably performed by John Gielgud, forever sitting at the head of an empty table stirring his tea and reading. Embarrassing an unwanted English guest by insisting that he was really an American. And welcoming back a prodigal son with little more than a raised eyebrow and 'Hello, you again. Been away haven't you? How long was it? Eighteen months? As long as that?' in a tone of voice suggesting the boy was free to leave immediately.

Then there was the *Good Soldier Schweik* on 0-28, putting

the other side of the coin. Contrasting the posturing pomposity of the aristocracy with the cunning and ingenuity of the peasant. Years ago I found myself in Prague at the same time as the Russian army where the only symbol of defiance left for the Czechs were little figures of the good soldier, either dangling from the rear vision mirrors of taxis, or plonked in meagre window displays in Wenceslas Square. The Russian thugs had obliterated the pro-Dubcek slogans and any other sign of ideological indiscipline. But they didn't seem to realise the subversive implications of these little dolls. Well, if anyone in Moscow saw the dazzling adaptation of Hasek's wonderful novel, they'd now know what that grinning, saluting buffoon is all about. And what he's about is thumbing his nose at tyranny. He's about surviving under the militarist's boot. In its obscenities and ironies, in its exuberance and satire, the *Good Soldier Schweik* was one of the great joys of television for me, and I can't wait for a rerun.

Also absent without leave is the company from *Hill Street Blues*, the cleverest, most original US series we've seen in years. The camera lurches through a chaotic police precinct in Chicago, following the adventures and misadventures of a brilliant company of cops, robbers and clowns in a programme that doesn't hesitate to flare in real anger or to recognise the complications and contradictions in the simplest human affairs. Much of what's best in American television derives from English models (the Norman Lear programme being inspired by series like *Till Death Us Do Part*) and I've no doubt that the *Hill Street Blues* people were influenced by *Z Cars* and *Softly Softly*. But in its depth and in the dazzling performances of writers, directors and actors alike, it stands proudly on its own. I look forward to a further series with yearning and impatience.

Then there's the jaw-slackening wonder of *Cosmos*, with Carl Sagan. While I could do without the soft-focus close-ups of Mr Sagan looking sensitive, it remains the most exhilarating documentary series in the history of the medium. Sagan scoops up a handful of sand and we watch the (approximately) 10,000 grains sifting through his fingers. He then tells us that there are more stars out there than there are grains of sand on *all* the beaches on *all* countries on Earth. In every programme there are, perhaps, a dozen such revelations that fill you with astonishment and awe. It's been the most exhilarating roller-coaster ride for the mind and feelings. If 0-28 can jolt us out of our ethnocentricity into an awareness of the wider world, *Cosmos* jars us out of our planetary provincialism, making us realise that we're but a fart in the big bang's windstorm.

From the sublime to the gore blimey. I am addicted, hopelessly and helplessly, to *Minder*. In my view Terry and Arthur, bovver boy and conman, are the most romantic duo since Nelson Eddy and Jeanette MacDonald. These counter-culture cockneys making a quid on the unofficial side of the British economy are one of the great joys of the cathode era.

Then there are one-off delights like *Jimmy Dancer*, a triumph for the ABC's drama department, in which Garry McDonald showed the human spirit coming to terms with malignancy, in a candid, compassionate and bravely comic dramatisation of perhaps our most lurking anxiety. Every bit as good as the best plays belted out by that extraordinary talent, Stuart Wagstaff, the greatest British playwright since William Shakespeare.

On and on the list goes, so don't tell me that telly should apologise for itself. It's taken us to the moon and the planets, to the bottom of the ocean, to the dawn of history and to the heights of folly. It has saved us from the tedium of conversation and, with the greatest respect to books, has given us things that books cannot provide. It has shown us images that Da Vinci, Michelangelo and Turner would have *died* to see. Whatever its sins of omission or commission, television is a triumph and I'm for giving Logie a Logie.

A recipe for Adams

I'm sure that all of you who collect recipes have tried that pièce de resistance of cordon noir, as presented by the three witches from Macbeth. 'Round about the cauldron go, in the poison'd entrails throw.' Just the thing when unexpected guests drop in. Well, this week I received something similar, posted by the parents or teacher of a little kid called Dionnie. Under the heading 'Phillip Adams Comes' it was written in a big, round hand with crayon'd illustrations.

> One day I was sitting on my
> bed reading a book and the
> book was about Magic.
> I was reading a magic
> recipe and I knew it couldn't
> be true but something made
> me try to make it.
> So I got out all of the thin-
> gs, pepper, a frog, some bacon,
> three eggs and a crayon.
> I mixed all of the things
> together in a big bowl and
> stirred continuasly
> suddenly something
> came out of the bowl.
> 'Oh', I said, 'if it isn't Phillip
> Adams.' I'm telling you I nearly died
> seeing him there.
> We were quiet for a few
> minutes.
> Then we started telling
> jokes about the hospital.
> It left
> me in stitches.

That night I thanked
Phillip Adams for coming.
When I was bored I just
made that spell and out of the
book would come Adams.
The only trouble was
I kept running out of frogs.

Gandhi — an *E.T.* for grown-ups

While applauding the timeliness of the message of *Gandhi*, I find it absurd that Attenborough's Anglo-Indian epic is being loaded down with Oscars. Apart from that reasonably spectacular second-unit work that Attenborough *didn't* direct, most of the film is visually ploddy, over-pretty and, worse still, grossly over-simplifies both Gandhi and the crises of Independence and Partition. Remove Ben Kingsley's worthy imitation of the Mahatma (and that of the Indian actor who plays the fierce and uncompromising Jinnah) and you've a series of dioramas that diminish the man and diffuse the issues.

Moreover I can't see where Attenborough spent his $20 million. A massive budget anywhere on earth, it would have been greatly magnified in India. Yet apart from the obligatory crowd scenes (all those free extras for the funeral scene, one of the most wasted opportunities in the history of cinema) the film was all too austere and simple. A man sitting around in a nappy, twirling a spinning wheel. One wonders how many rupees were spent lubricating the creaking machinery of Indian bureaucracy.

As a portrait of the Mahatma, the film was less than honest. Where were his sexual quirks? The scandals caused by his sleeping naked with young girls, including his granddaughters? His horror when he discovered, late in life, that he was still capable of having anatomical responses to erotic dreams? Where were his fanatical and foolish philosophies on diet? What of his disastrous rejection of western medicine? Or of his extraordinary suggestion that Britain should allow Hitler to occupy Great Britain? For all his goodness and guile (and I'm perfectly willing to accept Mountbatten's judgment that Gandhi was as great a man as Christ or Buddha), he was also a monumental and magnificent ratbag. And by giving us a pasteurised Gandhi, free of impurities and perversities, Richard Attenborough does his memory — and history — a disservice. Anxious not to offend the regime, he seems to have air-brushed out every blemish so that we see a saint instead of an erratic, eccentric, Machiavellian strategist.

Exploiting the coincidence of a surname, Madam Gandhi has much to gain from the domestic and international success of the movie. Yet in a very sad way the timing of the film's release emphasises the failure of Gandhi's dreams and ideals. When the film was picking up its accolades, communal violence was erupting in India. As the *Economist* reported: 'In Assam last month, Assamese Hindus killed Bengali Moslems, Assamese Moslems killed Bengali Moslems, tribals killed Assamese Hindus, tribals killed Bengali Moslems, tribals killed tribals, Bengali Moslems killed Bengali Hindus, older assimilated Bengali immigrants killed recently arrived ones, and all the local people killed Nepalese and Baharis. Every community turned on every other community.'

So much for the Mahatma's message. Partitions into Pakistan and Bangladesh notwithstanding, India is still torn apart by divisions in race, language, religion, class and caste. While his 'harijan' or Children of God are now guaranteed their place in government, the Untouchables are still brutalised and murdered when they get out of line. And for all of India's (and Indira's) efforts, the situation of its people still appals. Of the 23 million Indian babies born this year, 4 million will die in childhood and 9 million will suffer from serious physical and mental disabilities as a consequence of malnutrition. Another 7 million will suffer lesser forms of malnutrition with only 3 million becoming truly healthy adults. In other words, barely 15 per cent of Indian kids will be able to achieve their full potential.

To the tourist visiting India, whose senses reel at the country's beauty and variety, at the luscious imagery and contrasting landscapes, much of this is invisible. 'In a poor society most mothers think of their offspring as normal', says the *Economist*, 'Deficiencies of protein, iron and other minerals damage the brain and body metabolism like a cancer. There's a steady fall in the intake of protein among the poor. In India soya bean production is picking up but it is used mainly to feed cattle and poultry so that animals fatten while humans decay.'

The contradiction about untouchability (outlawed yet flourishing) is echoed in the attitude to women. India is ruled by a woman and yet females are discriminated against in the most terrible ways. For example, at meal times in countless villages, girls simply do not get an equitable share of the available protein. Among kids under five, girls have a 60 per cent higher incidence of third degree malnutrition. The tradition of female infanticide in parts of northern India may have been destroyed — yet female children still die through neglect.

To some extent Gandhi bears the responsibility for modern India. His political party, Congress, remains monstrously corrupt. His economic thoughts never developed beyond a Utopian form of agrarian revivalism which, as Zireer Masani accurately describes in the *New Statesman* 'blames the evils of modern science and technology for economic oppression, while exonerating India's feudal and propertied classes'. Gandhi was welcomed by the feudal landlords, the big businesses and even the princes because of his concept of 'trusteeship' which embraced them. It is crucial to remember that his campaigns on behalf of the under-privileged were *not* directed against their Indian oppressors but only against British capitalists and landlords. As Masani comments: 'The cause for which Gandhi is best remembered, the uplift of Untouchables, never went beyond symbolic gestures. Gandhi renamed them harijans or "children of God" and duly worshipped them; but he rejected their own efforts to organise politically, ignored the economic causes of their poverty and landlessness and even defended the Hindu caste system as an ideal division of labour, once purged of the taboo of untouchability.'

It should also be remembered that Gandhi used his non-violence techniques against any tendency to left-wing politics in India. Whenever the Left looked like taking up his civil disobedience campaigns, whenever it looked as though he, Gandhi, might lose the spotlight and therefore the power, the Great Soul would cancel them.

'In retrospect', writes Masani, 'the most negative aspect of Gandhi's legacy was the political tokenism and hypocrisy legitimised by his cult of poverty and his glorification of individual renunciation. As one of his more irreverent disciples remarked, it cost a lot to keep the Mahatma in poverty. His insistence on third class rail travel meant that a whole carriage had to be reserved for him, while his dietary and other fads meant that only the very rich could afford to have him as a house guest. The fetishes, which seem forgivable eccentricities in Gandhi himself, became a calculated hypocrisy with future generations of congressmen. In India today, a spotless Gandhi-cap and khaddar uniform are far more likely to evoke the whited sepulchres of Congress corruption than any commitment to non-violence.'

But back to the movie. Attenborough ignores Gandhi's attempts to be a dapper little Englishman, censors his extraordinary sexual behaviour, and tells us all sorts of white lies about his relationship with Nehru and his lieutenants. Far from being uncritical devotees of the Mahatma, they spent much of their time enraged by his calculated naivety and towards the time of Partition would cheerfully have throttled him. Equally the film glosses over the real tragedy of Gandhi's life — that his final months were full of bitterness and self-recrimination. Before his assassination he could see clear evidence that the Congress Party was going to degenerate into a power-hungry bun fight. He also recognised that he was being rejected by Nehru and that his dream of a united India had turned into a nightmare. While acknowledging that Attenborough didn't have time to fit everything into the film — from Gandhi's violin lessons to the Indian naval mutiny of 1946 — he had no excuse to leave out so much. I'm reminded of the audio-animatronic Abraham Lincoln that reads the Gettysburg Address at Disneyland. You do no service to history by turning politicians into gods, and, however exemplary he might have been, Gandhi was first and last a consummate politician.

Mind you, what can you expect when Mrs Gandhi was providing so much of the budget, personally vetting the screenplay and the film's final cut. The result is, in many ways, a piece of official art, little more convincing than the Kremlin's representations of Stalin as everyone's benign old uncle.

Let's look at some of Gandhi's more Pythonesque statements and beliefs — the qualities of paradox and contradiction that made him far more infuriating and remarkable than Attenborough's wartless hero.

When Mussolini overran Ethiopia, Gandhi urged the

Ethiopians to 'allow themselves to be slaughtered'. The result, he said, would be more effective than resistance since, after all, Mussolini didn't want a desert. Believing a similar conduct would 'convert the Germans to an appreciation of human dignity' he suggested that the British 'invite Hitler and Mussolini to take whatever they want of the countries you call your possessions . . . let them take possession of your beautiful island with its many beautiful buildings. You'll give all this, but neither your minds nor your souls.' Tell that to six million Jews.

As someone commented during the fight for independence, Gandhi was fortunate to confront the British, for all their sins, rather than the Germans. Or, for that matter, the Belgians whose record in the Congo suggests that pacifism would have been an absurdly inappropriate stance. In other words, passive resistance is a magnificent weapon when your enemy has a conscience.

And what of Gandhi's ludicrous hostility to western medicine? His wife died when Gandhi refused to allow a doctor to use a hypodermic needle. With a deep-rooted belief in 'natural cures' he disapproved of modern medicine's emphasis on the body's *physical* aspects 'at the expense of the spirit'. A hypodermic would, he argued, allow his wife's body to be subjected to violence. So she died in agony.

A few years later, his beloved great-niece Manu almost died of acute appendicitis. After days of agony in which Gandhi insisted on treating the poor child with mud packs, strict diet and enemas, he finally ('with the utmost reluctance') allowed her to be saved by the violence of a surgeon's scalpel.

Gandhi's sexual obsessions included his determination to shrink his sexual organ through diet. Through the proper intake of food, Gandhi believed he could 'lie by the side of even a Venus in all her naked beauty, without being physically or mentally disturbed'. After thirty years of discipline and prayer, he was convinced he'd achieved this lofty moral state — until an incident in Bombay in 1936 that he referred to as 'my darkest hour'. At the age of 67, thirty years after he'd sworn his vow of Brahmacharya, he arose after what a biographer describes as 'an arousing dream with what would have been to most men of that age a source of some satisfaction'. Namely, an erection.

He was so overwhelmed by anguish at 'this frightful experience' that he swore a vow of total silence for six weeks. Sex was to remain a constant preoccupation and, from time to time, a source of scandal for the Great Soul — yet there's not the slightest hint of it in Attenborough's movie.

There are so many things missing from the Attenborough version. Where is Gandhi's tragic relationship with his own children? Where are the maharajahs of Princely India who, having sided with the British, helped turn Partition into such a monstrous jigsaw? Where is the contribution of Mountbatten and the heroism of Edwina, his wife? What of Churchill's undying hatred of the 'half naked fakir'? And shouldn't the record show that it was a British *Labor* Government that determined to end colonial rule? And where's the admission that it was a fellow Hindu, albeit a Hindu fascist, who assassinated Gandhi? And why is Vallabhbhia Patel, the 'toecutter' of New Delhi politics, depicted as a sort of amiable buffoon? Sins of omission and commission abound, so that when I described *Gandhi* as an *E.T.* for grown-ups in this column a few weeks ago, I wasn't entirely joking. The way Attenborough and Spielberg have approached their material, their central characters are so sentimentalised as to be interchangeable.

Claustrophobia

Thanks to phollowers of Sigmund Phreud, we know of a wide variety of phobias.

There's Gamophobia, the fear of marriage. Optophobia, the fear of opening one's eyes. Astraphobia, Keraunophobia, Ceraunophobia and Tonitrophobia, being four different names for the fear of thunder. The text books record something called Arachibutyrophobia, being the fear of peanut butter sticking to the roof of the mouth. And there's Baccilophobia, as suffered by Howard Hughes and ladies in Pea Beu commercials, being the fear of microbes.

But the phobia of phobias, more common than Ergophobia, the fear of work, and more understandable than Thanatophobia, the dread of death, comes CLAUSTROPHOBIA, being an overwhelming revulsion towards Christmas. Its full Latin name is, of course, Santaclaustrophobia, and around this time of year the symptoms are intolerable. I keep hearing 'Jingle Bells' and feel I'm being followed by a red-nosed reindeer.

Nonetheless I shall choke back my distaste and write the obligatory nostalgia column on the subject of Yule.

Now, what's a non-Christian like myself (I hear you ask) doing discussing Christmas? Well, the fact is that Christmas isn't. Christian, that is. You see, the Christians pinched it from those decadent pagans, the Romans. For centuries they celebrated Saturnalia on 7 December, which was a time for 'merry making and the exchanging of gifts'. And in Roman New Year, when houses were decorated with greenery and little oil lamps, still more gifts were given out, to children and the poor. Moreover 25 December was regarded as the birth date of the Iranian mystery god, Mithra, the Sun of Righteousness. So I've written to the Ayatollah Khomeiny urging him to sue the Myer Emporium for breach of copyright.

In any case, despite the claustrophobia that's afflicted me in adult years, I've happy memories of the season from my childhood in East Kew, when an up-ended pillow case disgorged its pile of separate gifts, each shrouded in its holly or sleigh-printed paper.

Which is a good time to make the point that a Christmas stocking wasn't. A stocking, that is. While illustrations of Chrissie always had Santa hanging brimming socks from the post of the bed, most kids retrieved their prezzos from bulging pillow cases. After all, apart from the odd League ruckman, who had socks that big? As for the new-fangled nylons, no woman was going to waste one of those desirable wisps on some dubious tradition.

The only leg-shaped receptacles were the ones bought from shops, made from lurid red mesh. These could only have been the stockings of dwarf-sized chorus girls. Stapled to cardboard, they contained really *grotty* gifts like inedible lollies, squashed party hats, Heckle and Jeckle comics, razor-sharp, frog-shaped 'clickers', very small packs of squashed plasticine, a torn Lone Ranger mask and a bent cardboard trumpet.

Now technology has come to the rescue with panty-hose, which must represent a considerable breakthrough. For here, combined with a remarkable potential for stretching, are not one but *two* legs connected to a single gusset. In other words, prezzos in stereo.

But back to the up-ended pillow case. There we were, confronted with the delicious dilemma of what parcel to open first. I took the view that large, soft presents tended to be boring things like clothing and so got them out of the way first, leaving the harder, heavier little parcels for After.

I can remember the way my grandma would urge me to remove the paper carefully, so that it could be used to wrap presents next year, a ritual still observed in our family where we retain race-memories of the Depression. (As a result we've got drawers stuffed as tightly as any turkey with ancient accumulations of rather torn and tatty wrappings that are no more likely to be recycled than grandma's Lan-Choo coupons are to be redeemed.)

So you'd open those squashy parcels first, feigning enthusiasm for a new pair of winceyette pyjamas or half a dozen singlets. And then, at last, it was into the real stuff — revealing a Colt .45 cap pistol with a plastic pearl handle that you'd seen in the toy shop window and nagged your mum about for months. Or a Dinky car with little removable tyres that were lost within the hour. Or a Meccano set with red and green girders from which you made aeroplanes with the aeronautic potential of bricks. Or a Hornby clockwork set that could be used for spectacular level-crossing smashes with the aforementioned Dinky car. Or the latest Richmal Crompton volume, *William Holds His Own*, undoubtedly the apotheosis of British literature. Or the new woggle (or was it a toggle?) for your cub uniform.

I well remember my first cowboy suit, made up of a little leather waistcoat with tassels, and strange bandy-things called chaps. According to subsequent researches, they were a reasonably accurate representation of authentic cowboy apparel — sort of aprons for legs, designed to prevent wear and tear as you rode through the cactus. However, because of their ridiculous appearance, they faded quickly from popularity. Indeed, they even disappeared from Western movies, along with those absurdly over-sized cowboy hats affected by Tom Mix. However there was one year in which almost every kid in East Kew was seen waddling around in chaps, going ksssh ksssh at each other with loaded fingers, or highly-plated Colt .45 cap pistols with plastic bone handles. They came and went like the mini. Within a couple of years they'd had the chop. Chaps had cashed their chips.

(In some ways the best prezzos were less orthodox and often second-hand. There were the badges that uncles gave you to stick on a beret that, just before you lost it, was so *encrusted* with metallic mementos that it out-weighed the Imperial crown. Or the battered hand-wound gramophone somebody gave you so that you could play wireless stations, endlessly announcing your two 78s, being 'I Did But See Her Passing By And Yet I'll Love Her Till I Die' and one with Crosby Morrison introducing the humourless laughter of the kookaburra.)

After you'd unwrapped your presents it was customary to go out and explore the near-by streets, trying to see what the other kids had got. John Sinclair, who lived in a *brick* house with an inside toilet, in contrast to your dilapidated weatherboard with its teetering sentry box, would be almost certain to have a new scooter with a foot brake or a two-wheeler with gears. Up the street the athletic David Preston would be skiting with his pneumatic Denzel Don Match II footy, with its fragrant scent of freshly burnished hide. Across the road, a couple of ringlet'd sisters, apparently cloned by their adoring mother from Shirley Temple, would be venturing forth with new dolls that woke, walked and even widdled. While up in Violet Grove there was a kid whose dad, being a builder, built the best billy carts in the business — long low numbers with screaming ball-bearing wheels.

We'd all look at each other's prezzos with envy and avarice and there'd be tentative transactions like 'You can have a shoot with my cap pistol if I can have a ride on your cart.'

Thinking back to childhood, I can remember almost every gift I received. I can check them off in my mind, year by year. The tin drum, the balsa-wood glider kit, the crystal set, the Snakes and Ladders and Draughts sets, the Boys and Girls Own Annuals (stories about Billy Bunter and Fortiscue-Smythe from the Upper Fifth, full of references to mysterious things called dorms, and fags that weren't cigarettes) and a bamboo fishing rod that was used on a single uneventful trip to the nearby Yarra. Ah, that beautiful stretch of willows that has long since disappeared beneath the F-19 Freeway.

The contrast with today is both dramatic and depressing. Modern kids are buried in a glut of gifts, in things that whir, blink and even speak. Where our weaponry was limited to the cap pistol, water pistol, spud gun and bow and arrow (for years I thought they were called 'bone arrows'), the modern kid has an arsenal worthy of the Pentagon, employing the same state-of-the-art circuitry. And I suspect that the same sort of technological advancement that's turned a cap pistol into a Space War laser gun has also wreaked havoc on the simplicity of the sleeping doll. Instead of little moans of 'Mumma' and the odd drop of micturition, I presume the new wave dolls are capable of enjoying copulation and suffering from toxic shock.

Only a few weeks ago I saw one with a motorised mouth that actually ingested fluid from a little plastic bottle. When the teet was removed, you'd have sworn the thing was auditioning for Deep Throat.

For the next few weeks the floors of Australia will not be safe for adult feet. We will walk through a minefield of expensive play things left strewn by our sated siblings. And you won't be able to look at your telly because of the relentless advance of Space Invaders, blurting their electric raspberries as they march down the screen. Within a week the whole lot will be broken, flat-batteried or malfunctioning and will be lying amongst the beggar's velvet beneath their beds or buried under shoes in the bottom of wardrobes.

I'm picking up the last few prezzos this morning. There's a very nice junior drug addict's kit at the local store, complete with a cute little heroin syringe, although the youngest is opting for a Kama Sutra Barbi ('See all the fun positions for Barbi and Ken!') The oldest wants her own computer 'to help with my homework, daddy'. But the one she's after comes with a programme that says 'Turn Mum and Dad into helpless robots'.

All things considered, I hope that the Strategic Air Command shoots Santa down with a heat-seeking missile as soon as he lifts out of his silo in the North Pole. At very least, we should spray Agent Orange over any mistletoe or holly and lay baits for Donner and Blitzen. And considering the expense of prezzos (not to mention the inevitable invasion of rellos) I'm for giving 25 December back to the Iranians.